PRENATAL YOGA
& Natural Birth

Jeannine Parvati Baker

PRENATAL YOGA
& Natural Birth

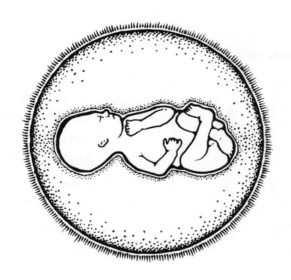

NORTH ATLANTIC BOOKS, BERKELEY, CALIFORNIA
FREESTONE PUBLISHING COMPANY, MONROE, UTAH

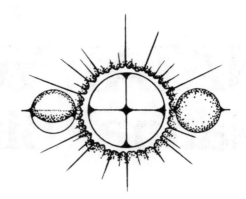

Prenatal Yoga and Natural Birth

Copyright © 1974, 1986
by Jeannine Parvati Baker

ISBN 0–938190–89–X

12th Printing 1984
New Edition 1986

Publishers' Addresses:

North Atlantic Books
2800 Woolsey Street
Berkeley, California 94705

Freestone Publishing Company
P.O. Box 398
Monroe, Utah 84754

Cover art © 1974 by Phoenix and Arabeth.
Airbrushed color added 1986 by Lloyd
Nelson, Four Corner Graphics

Book design and most drawings done
originally by the author, later enhanced
and expanded by Max Efroym

Illustrations © 1974 by Max Efroym,
Fish Creek Studios

Book design of 1986 edition by
Paula Morrison

Photo credits:

Jeannine Parvati Baker: 11, 19, 62–66, 73,
  75, 79, 80, 84. 87, 89, 92, 96.

Rico Baker: 86, 87, 88, 91.

Bruce Berger: 72.

G. Franzen: 2, 13, 17, © 1974.

Reggie Henkart: 7, 8, 67, 71, 93.

Michael Medvin: 16, 22–59.

Vicki O'Brien: 68.

Kristina Wilcox: 14, 60, 83, 94.

Prenatal Yoga and Natural Birth is sponsored
in part by the Society for the Study of Native
Arts and Sciences, a nonprofit educational
corporation whose goals are to develop an
ecological and crosscultural perspective link-
ing various scientific, social, and artistic
fields; to nurture a holistic view of arts,
sciences, humanities, and healing; and to
publish and distribute literature on the relationship of mind, body, and nature.

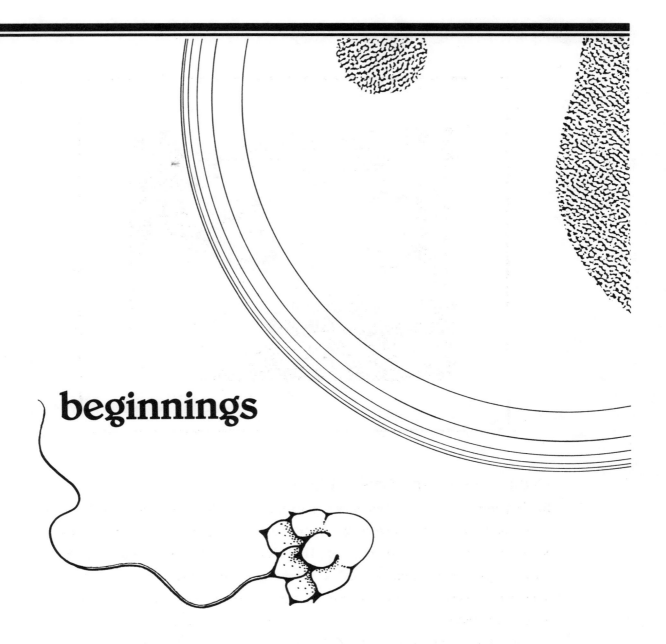

beginnings

I would like to dedicate this manual to several persons who inspired me and offered support with love. It is from a very tender place that I thank my love-child Loi Caitlin Medvin, the twin babies I now carry within my womb, Billy Prange, Lester & Bill Hazell, Stephanie, Carol, Ed, and Eugene from *Two Births*, Sat Nam Kaur from Tara, the Temple of the Divine Mother, my friend and publisher Robert Greenway, Rosalyn (Lolly) Ferrick my editor, and Phoenix 'n Arabeth, the artist who created the front and back covers. Also, special thanks to Gerald Franzen, our photographer friend and to Judy Rosales Levore, the beautiful model for most of the yoga photos. In addition, I feel great gratitude to all my pregnant students with whom I shared the experience of Prenatal Yoga.

Dedication To the New Edition

By my parents grace, I am here now writing this new dedication to the second edition of *Prenatal Yoga and Natural Birth*. Frank and Vicki O'Brien answered my call to come here and I am thankful they did. They also gifted me with a blood-sister whom I love dearly as well, Francine "Kit" O'Brien. Having only one blood-sister, I sometimes imagine I became a midwife in order to create many blood-sisters. To these sisters and my family of friends, I also dedicate this book.

We all come to this world through a woman by a man. Within each of us is our mother and father, represented in all cells by genes from both parents. In our psyches, the primal woman and man, are the inner feminine and masculine imprints of the soul.

Yoga balances all. How we carry our mother and father within from the cellular, to the psychological, can be made more graceful through yoga practice.

Perhaps then we can LIVE in a balanced way and our relationships will reflect this inner harmony. All polarities find their union within; and yoga equals union.

However yoga provides no guarantees. Just as huffing and puffing at birth doesn't necessarily create a blissful delivery, yoga makes no claim that its practice will insure liberation from all suffering. Always God's grace is the unknown yet vital insurance. However, conscious breathing does help conscious birth as does a devoted

yoga practice bring us a little closer to our source.

I dedicate this new edition to mothers and fathers who are committed to freedom through householding, i.e., realizing family as a spiritual practice. The world has seen a few examples of enlightened saints—perhaps now is the time for enlightened families.

To my family, in process of liberation, I give my fullest gratitude. To my husband, Vishnu Dass (Frederick Hamilton Baker), goes special appreciation. Without him, my balancing act on all levels would suffer. Rico, as I like to call my best friend, is also my wisest guru, my vulnerability and my inspiration.

To my children, Loi Caitlin, Oceana Violet, Cheyenne Coral, Gannon Hamilton and Quinn Ambriel—eternal devotion. I am blessed to have you in my life and down to the bone-seed know we have always been together and always will, through changing forms and all.

To all my unborn children I dedicate this book so that you might love our future world as a place of peace. Let this planet be known throughout the universe as holy ground, where there is true reverence for life.

Preface To the Second Edition
Welcome to the new edition of *Prenatal Yoga*.

This is my first book and like all original, creative projects, it occupies a tender place in my heart; the same way a first-born is special for breaking new ground. This book was the premiere guide on yoga and pregnancy/birth. Now there are many good titles to choose from which instruct mothers in yoga. This one was the first book and as some of you tell me, the best loved one.

    Prenatal Yoga has stood the test of time. In terms of the practices, there is nothing new. Truth needs no update. I wrote *Prenatal Yoga* when pregnant with my twins and felt somewhat unfinished even then with this book. My fantasy was to add the amazing birth stories of my twins. However the post-partum was more than a full-time job and *Prenatal Yoga* went to press with but one birth story.

    That was twelve years ago. Since that time I've become even more in awe of the ordinary miracle we call birth. I know less in some ways now than I did with my "beginner's mind." Four more babies have come through me since the first edition of *Prenatal Yoga*. Many more babies have emerged through my friendship circle and as midwife I've come to TRUST THE MYSTERY more.

Birth, being life's central metaphor, like yoga, provides an opportunity for higher consciousness, for enlightenment. The more we focus on the details, the clearer the big picture becomes. Birth is a hologram. A "holoerotic" (my lover calls it) experience which magnifies our essence, literally showing us the stuff we're made of. It's in the details that we find God. Looking closely at birth, we see ALL.

WE GIVE BIRTH AS WE CONCEIVE. I have added some conscious conception stories along with the birth tales of my babies. The new frontier for students of the perinatal process is conscious conception. A conscious conception is the cornerstone of holistic health and indeed fuller Self-awareness. As midwife I can best prepare families for natural birth if conscious conception is likewise natural in the family. Please refer to our title *Conscious Conception: Elemental Journey Through the Labyrinth of Sexuality* for more information on this spiritual practice.

Perhaps it is due to the nature of sexuality itself that most "spiritual paths" get tricky when integrating fertility. It seems especially so in yoga practices. When sexual energy is separated from reproduction it is easy for it to get kinky. Many "tantric yogis" get stuck and do not experience a balance of energy throughout their entire being. Making babies doesn't assure one of balanced chakras (wheels of energy, power centers located by major nerves and glands throughout the inner topology of our bodies), either. But separating spirituality, sex and fertility is a false division to begin with. Add the high value placed on celibacy by many spiritual paths and we have, rather than liberation, another even more confused situation complete with all the symptoms found in our larger culture of imbalance and irreverence for life.

Practicing yoga during pregnancy is one way to heal this split between soul and spirit. Prenatal yoga sexualizes spirituality and spiritualizes fertility. It is THE tantric practice of mothers. Once the babies come planetside, our yoga practice shifts into karma yoga beyond belief. We become servants to our babies and our path is bhakti yoga, the practice of devotion.

The wound reveals the cure, so says HYGIEIA, goddess of health. Combining yoga with natural birth as a sexual AND spiritual expression invites parents into an experience of co-creation. Healing one mother is healing our Earth. It allows us the possibility of realizing "the Garden" is here again and by naturally, ecstatically birthing babies that we are indeed bringing Heaven to Earth. Could this be the time when together we can fall into the HEART?

Writing as a latter-day feminist, my personal testimony is that better birthing equals better sexuality of all kinds. No longer is there a basis for fathers to be threatened by their wives practicing yoga and giving spontaneous birth—they see the radiant results. A woman at peace with her childbearing self is more likely to be at peace with her marital/sexual relationship as well. Traumatic births are negative reinforcements for sexual union. Healing one aspect of fertility tends to heal them all. Realizing birth as a SPIRITUAL as well as a NATURAL rite of passage opens up higher consciousness in all matters of transition, change and emergence.

Giving birth is initiation into women's mysteries. Like all good shamanic (spiritual) paths, it prepares us for other altered states and dying to the self. Giving conscious birth is woman's vision quest, par excellence. It is ultimate sadhana, spiritual practice, requiring purity in strength, flexibility, health, concentration, surrender and faith. Opening for conscious birth helps all power centers to open, especially the healing power of sexuality. Along with delivering babies, we open our hearts. (More on this in a forthcoming title, PSYCHE'S MIDWIFE.)

Taking drugs to numb birthforce sensations lays the imprint to "feel-not" other sexual experiences. It gives a negative example to our children. The imprint for the medicated baby at delivery is to need drugs whenever faced with movement into new territory. We have entire generations taking drugs to document this idea that the birth imprint (perhaps conception too) lays down powerful patterns, tasks for a lifetime to make conscious and change, if so desired.

Conceptions become less holy without unmedicated births to balance them. Though more and more births are unmedicated amongst the underground illuminati, it might seem that conceptions rarely are. So many of us ourselves were born anesthetized, drugged senseless. Therefore our imprint when facing primal sexuality and co-creation is to turn to drugs again like our sources did. We conceive as we birth.

If we didn't need medical help in conceiving our babies, we don't need it at delivery. We CAN change these deepest imprints and transcend the deadening rituals of our culture by giving birth consciously. For our future's sake, let us give an example of doing what is best-for-life right from the beginning.

Taking the full responsibility is risky—as is all life a risk. Yet the ability to respond (responsibility) to life emerging, empowers us tremendously. None of us get out of here alive anyway, says the dominant mythology of mortalists, so the bigger risks for the bigger games.

However myths, like dreams, change as the culture changes and we are learning that ECSTASY IS INDEED WORTH MORTALITY. Our collective waking dream is allowing conception and birth to now become fully the sacred rites of passage they always were, and are.

Included herein are four more birth stories, testimonies to my sacred ecstasy. Looking back on each delivery, I see my progress in assisting the birthforce. My fifth

birth ("The Dolphin Midwife") was holy orgasmic! I compare it with my first birth "Emergence" of Loi's unmedicated, intact hospital birth, unfairly I suppose. Yet I recall how relatively less orgasmic I was the first time I made love, as compared to where I am now. So it is with giving birth—ecstasy comes with practice. The same in spiritual practices of yoga—we can "stand outside ourselves" (the original meaning of ecstasy) with more practice. Through sadhana, ecstasy grows for us mothers who love our calling with a passion.

MEETING WHAT COMES FULLY is one of the goals of yoga (santosha, contentment)—and it is the best advice in childbirth as well. With breath as ally we can receive a vision which will spiritually feed us our entire lives, right at the moment of birth (and conception). Go into the intensity, up to the very edge of eternity. Open to the stretch of body/mind, knowing each moment for what it is. Be thankful for life however it presents itself. RECEIVE THE BLESSINGS OF BIRTH GENTLY AND IN LOVE.

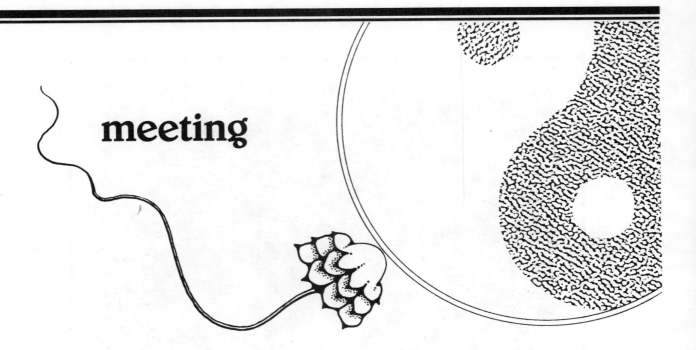

meeting

This book has a history rooted in women's mythology and yoga. The story goes like this—A Marin County housewife traveled to India to study yoga with a master. While practicing, she became pregnant and shared the news with her teacher who told her that now she would have to stop. She replied that yoga was her path and that she didn't want to stop. It seemed to her that during pregnancy yoga was especially important as she needed the strength and suppleness to handle these new and powerful feelings and levels of consciousness brought about by being pregnant. (The literature refers to this phenomenon as "emotional lability," the seeming madness of normal pregnancy. Being pregnant alters one's consciousness and in the realm of emotions this manifests as intense mood changes.)

I can merely conjecture as to the reasons this wise man advised his student to stop practicing yoga. Perhaps he too was inculcated with the general mystique of pregnancy. Pregnancy is viewed by many incapable of experiencing it (and even by some who do) as something not O.K., or at the very least a nine-month suspension from the real business of living a regular life. The same attitude is sometimes tragically employed in the raising of children by parents on a definite spiritual path: that these years of caring for children are somehow distracting them from their spiritual evolution. I know that this is illusion—our daughter has been our greatest teacher and living with her has provided ample opportunity to see how high we really are. And so it is with pregnancy. Now, you may wonder why pregnancy might conflict with yoga. I believe it is due to the inappropriateness of traditional Hatha Yoga on one very basic level: it doesn't feel good. A yoga more in tune with the Great Moon Force, of a more

cyclical nature and one of changing flow is far more beneficial for woman embodying the most exaggerated form of the female principle. And so (to return to our wandering pregnant housewife) her teacher heard this and responded with tremendous ability and helped instruct his student in modifications of yoga for pregnancy. Eastern man and western woman together began the discipline of prenatal yoga. Where we all catch glimpses and sometimes really *know* the true path is in the integration of our sun and moon forces, dark and light, strength and fluidity. A balance, a union.

Discipline is very much needed during pregnancy, not only from the ritual aspect, but to prepare for the great discipline required in caring for a baby. You can choose daily whether to do prenatal yoga or not—but you *have* to "do" a baby every day. This was of course my preference, yet there were some days when the centering practices I had developed in yoga sustained me through crying spells and teething. The synthesis of these traditional disciplines and my student's teachings and my experiences in natural childbirths is what I want to share with you in this manual. It is an offering made with love and the knowledge that you, pregnant person, are truly the Grace of God.

Namaste and happy yoga!

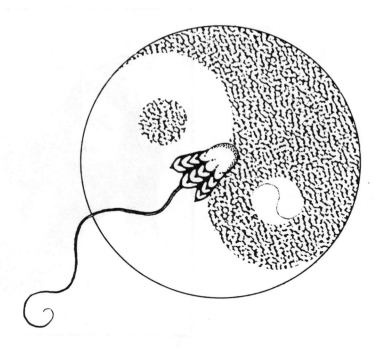

for you, gentle mother

Moments after Loi was born, we were enveloped in a cosmic imprinting experience of tremendous energy. There was no way Loi would be separated from me and we sucessfully realized this continuation of our oneness through hospital regimentation and inhumanities. Only 6 pounds, the staff wanted to place Loi in a "warmer"—I explained that my body was quite warm enough. Six hours after Loi's emergence, we were hitchhiking home to Sonoma County from San Francisco. Together, intensely bonding, realizing, delighting in one another's presence. I learned in these first few critical hours how to be gentle, tender, attuned to my baby. Loi was my teacher as I was hers and I learned well how to love unconditionally. I will say to you that your baby will illuminate more of yourself, show you your limitations and your strengths, than you can now imagine. Babies are continual pulsing manifesta-

tions of here/now rhythms. Babies look like Budhas—behave like one total attachment. And the attachment is to your titty—nursing continues the flow of nourishment and pleasure begun within your body via placenta. Loi bagan mursing one half hour after birth and didn't disengage (or so it seemed) for months. She has just turned four and is newly weaned. Our nursing experience was unusually long for this culture but just right for us. Breastfeeding is an intimate, pleasurable, sexual experience and as such it is completely unique for each couple involved.

Having babies is having hope. And giving up the struggle, to return again to the magic of protoplasm forming, emerging a sentient being, a baby, a girl-child, a woman, a grandmother. I am mothering my daughter in a different consciousness than I was mothered twenty years ago. We raise our daughters far more differently than a mere twenty-year span would indicate. My daughter says, "I know my body"—I am still engaging in many therapies to re-know mine. She knows what she wants and generally how to go about fulfilling her needs. I believe this comes from mothering that is symbiotic in a sense—our needs are mutually fulfilled in the process. Mothering needn't be a duty. It is a preference and a pleasure if these few

things are kept in mind and soul: be not afraid to touch, naked body to naked body, to sleep with your baby, to nurse very often and orgasmically, to feel your own pain, anger and frustrations and and express them as purely as your baby will. Tune into your own *mother within* for nourishment and reach out for help from other aquarian mothers. Support one another as you gently support your babies. We are all growing up together. And so, calm-pond of a woman that you are, what if you have given birth to a fire-child that cries and cries? What do you want, your fantasized baby of perfection or your real one here with you now? I was so attached to my ideals of *happy baby* that I felt much pain in the tearing away of those visions of quiet easy mothering so I could respond to my crying, fretting baby. I took solace that crying brought oxygen to her growing brain. Good! She will be smart but gosh! what a way to intelligence. I'd have gladly traded for a less bright,

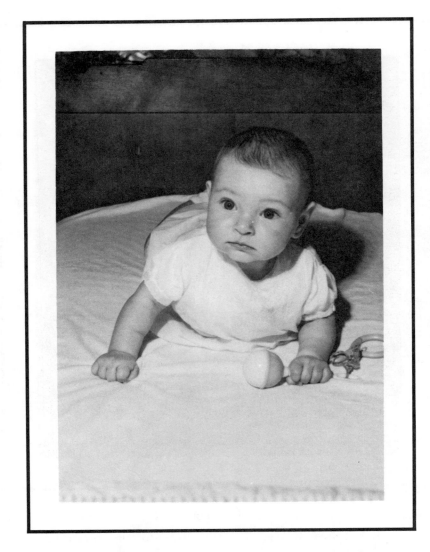

"sleepy" baby some days. My own mother held onto her fantasy so tight of what I should be like that she became uptight and would not allow her milk to flow. Let go of fantasies. Your baby demands total responsiveness to who she is now. A baby is very real, if you'll let her be. And she will teach you compassion and patience, and what is *really* important in life.

How *can* we prepare ourselves best for a flowing childbirth and mothering/nursing experience? Reading many books (intellectual preparation), hanging out with happy mothers and babies like at La Leche League meetings (social preparation), practicing prenatal yoga (spiritual preparation), and attending natural childbirth classes (physiological preparation) are all integral to an excellent preparation—yet, if we still carry the tissue tensions of our unfelt pains,

our trauma in being born and being mothered, these will act as obstacles to feeling the joyful, natural rhythms in becoming a family. During my first daughter's childbirth experience, I encountered fifteen minutes or so of fear, tension, and pain and found myself assuming the martyr's posture. Michael, with his very aware coaching, gently pointed out that I appeared nailed to the cross—in fact, I looked just like the heroine we had seen together in a movie years earlier who had nobly suffered to give birth. When I really heard that, I could give up that persona and return to my center. The image of suffering to give birth was imprinted in me not only at the "bigger than life silver screen" experiences of movies, but from my own emergence from my mother (at her birth). A few good yells to release my tension, express my felt pain, and the flood of programs from my past being made conscious, worked far better to relax my body/self than any medication being offered by the nurse. For to take drugs during childbirth is to continue the deadening vicious cycle that makes non-feeling persons in our

culture. Allen Cohen said that if all men could help their children
into this world and see them emerge from their women, there would
be no more wars. I would add that if babies were born naturally,
undrugged, uncircumcized, in tune to their own rhythms from whole
(connected, feeling, untraumatized by episiotomies and non-loving
attendants) women—there would be no violence at all. The children
of our new age would be able to give up our competitive, struggling,
violence program for there would be no place of disconnected,
un-felt pain from which to "act out" and hurt others (ourselves).
And it is for this main reason that I have shared this book with
you, my gentle sister.

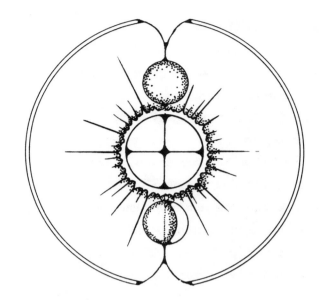

going through

You Are Pregnant, Vessel for New Life

The circle continues to revolve, the river continues to flow, the natural cycle of life, death and re-birth is unfolding. Your baby will come through you and not for you. Your participation in life's oldest ritual will be totally conscious and yet you will retain non-attachment, the flow. You are creatively expressing yourself in how you are pregnant. Being pregnant is not *for* your childbirth experience. Being pregnant is living here and now, this moment. Childbirth is just another moment you will transcend. Yoga is a practice, yours if you wish, to allow you delight in being alive right now.

Now focus on your breath. Inspire . . . let go . . . inspire . . . let go . . . a circle . . . you describe . . . with your breath . . . prana . . . primal life-force . . . when you exhale, let go of all the tension in your body . . . pretend there is a faucet in your navel and all your tension flows out of this faucet . . . breathe rhythmically, evenly, as slow and relaxed as you can. Feel the breath in all living things (ever listen to a plant breathe?). Listen to your own breath . . . (ajapna mantram) . . . listen as you read for a while. Breath is as vital a nutrient as vegetables you have grown yourself. Oxygen feeds your baby, allows your largest muscle, your uterus, to grow. And prana nourishes your two souls.

And So We Begin

Find a space for yourself—uninterrupted by the snaring traps life sometimes creates to entrap us. You are creating your own myth right now, living your karmic script and programs. One hour each day of free space, in warmth (preferably in the sun and fresh air), and a quiet place is needed for prenatal yoga. This yoga is truly a dance and you will want to explore several levels so make sure that your environment is comfortable for squatting, standing, kneeling, on hands and knees, and/or laying down flaked out. If you have response-abilities that make one hour daily too much to devote to practicing prenatal yoga, rewrite your adventure to allow this one hour to being present, mind and body united.

Find a place of power for you. A place in your garden where you feel especially centered and good, or in your living room. Be gentle with yourself. Each moment of prenatal yoga holds wisdom for you if you'll allow yourself to relax and not judge progress. Focus on how you feel rather than how you look. Delight in yourself, in meditative movement and the dance you are creating. The transition movements are as important as the asanas (postures) and entirely your own; make them graceful, flowing, meaningful—your own ritual.

Stand tall feeling your tailbone being drawn to the center of the earth by gravity, to the origin of the kundalini power within you. Simultaneously, feel the top of your head being drawn upwards and expanding

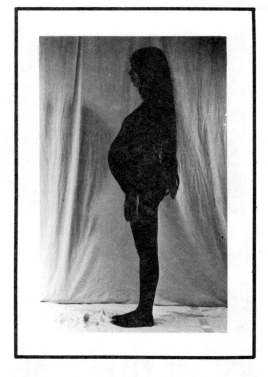

in all directions. Rock back and forth slowly feeling the line of gravity and the precise instant of the change-over from one leg to another. This will help you locate your center. Pretend that your legs are roots of a mighty tree and are firmly grounding you to mother earth. Again, return to your center (which changes as the earth revolves, stars rise and pregnancy progresses) and activate your center. For a moment feel your boundaries as an organism, feel your skin breathe, and notice how you confine yourself. Slow yourself down—be aware of your mind chattering and let thoughts go as you exhale all tension from your being. When you feel calm, begin with the first asana. . .

Neck Rolls

Pretend there is a beam of white light coming out of the top of your head and as

you revolve your head you create a circle
of white light around you. Your neck will
make many sounds if you roll slowly and
consciously, a cacophony of stories—some
the freeing of energy and some the crackling of tension released. Calcium deposits
and gases, and nerves, muscles, ligaments,
blood and bones are being pleasurably
massaged all over. We have to start at the

neck, for being women we hold lots of
inhibitory trips in our throats—little girls
don't shout so millions of screams are held
in our throats and our necks hold much
(formerly) unconscious tension which it
is necessary to encounter at the beginning
of yoga practice.

Balance is vital for yoga so if you roll
your neck seven times to the left, balance
that with equal revolutions to the right. And
do this very slowly, even slower, smoother
with the spirit of dance. No calisthenic-
consciousness. You are in grace and therefore truly graceful. Your breath is natural
and relaxed—feel the relaxation spread down
your shoulders so that you are wearing your
shoulders like a cape. Your arms hang freely
and they too are limp with relaxation. Feel
your breath travel down to your fingertips.
When you wear no armor at your neck, the
kundalini raised by your yoga practice will
pass freely up you spine to the top of your
head. This is realization of your inherent
progesterone bliss.

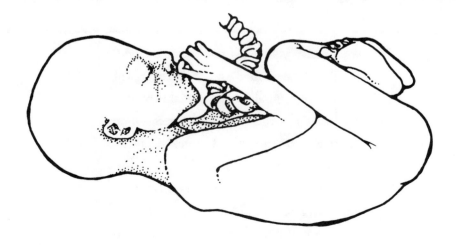

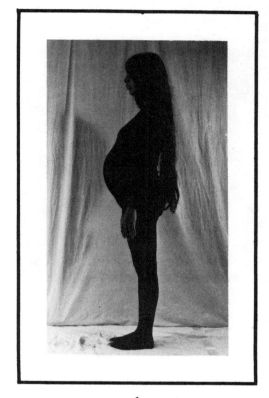

1

2

Folding to Squat

Gently come to a stop and balance your head directly over your axis. Begin inspiration through your nose and carefully, slowly drop your head by allowing your neck muscles to let go and continue dropping your head while exhaling through your mouth, lips loose and relaxed. Feel your spine—vertebra by vertebra—following the lead of your head down toward your feet while you exhale deeply (as deeply as you previously inhaled) until your hands, then your palms touch the ground. Your arms up to this moment have been dangling freely. Now you will use your arms to support your body and rest here on all fours, [3] weight equally distributed between your hands and feet while you let your uterus hang loose. Bend your knees to avoid placing any stress on the backs of your knees. Now you are inhaling deeply through your nose and when you've finished begin to lower yourself [4] into a squat by bending your knees. End up in a squat, knees in your armpits, legs open as you are open, feet as parallel as possible [5].

3 Squat Passive

Feel the life flow, for this posture is a bio-energetic one—the natural grooving position. Soon your hands and feet will be warm to the touch, warm with the flow of energy. Focus on your heartbeat and allow blood to permeate all your tissue. Imagine that blood now carries oxygen to your baby and that you have a window into your womb and can see pulsing placenta nourish and sustain, blood-bringing life to baby . . . a totally together universe manifested in the space of your uterus.

4

5

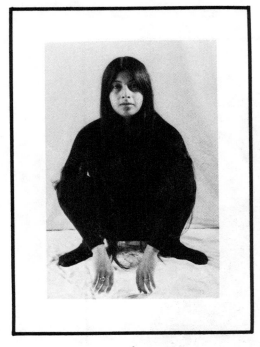

1

2

Squatting is the natural posture of rest and composure. People all over the world squat easily and women all over the world have babies easily and painlessly. Western pregnant women tend to sit in chairs, often with legs crossed, thus strengthening sets of ligaments that are the opposite of an open pelvis. If you must sit in chairs, draw your legs up in the half lotus posture of hatha yoga or "tailor-style" or comfortably up higher than your hips with your pelvic floor open. Sitting in a chair with your legs crossed is psychologically the posture of closed "ladies" and to have a baby one must be an open woman.

Now place your thumbs [2] ever so lightly on either side of the bridge of your nose. Slowly apply pressure by bringing your thumbs toward one another. This opens up your sixth chakra, and if you extend your fingers somewhat like antennae, you will stimulate the 72,000 nadis—sort of the "nerve" network of your *aura* (some call it *soul,* others call it an electro-magnetic field) that surrounds and complements and corresponds with the nervous system of our physical bodies. This mudra reportedly relieves headaches sometimes by allowing tears to flow. Place your palms over your eyes wide open [3] so that you see darkness —heels of hands placed on cheekbones, fingers holding forehead. Rest your eyes, the muscles around your eyes. This is a mudra that can be integrated into the yoga of living daily—between chapters of books, upon awakening (especially good for unraveling dreams).

3

4

Dreams: stories with secrets essentially for you to discover. As the hormone of pregnancy, progesterone, alters your consciousness, so do your dreams take on new levels of meaning. Dream about having your baby—women dream all situations for their upcoming childbirth experience: giving birth magically, realistically in color and naturally, giving birth to kittens, chimpanzees, avatars, our mothers, monsters, and a loaf of french bread all buttered and sliced. Listen to your dreams, dance them, paint them, play with them, finish them, live them. Then on to bigger things.

You have been squatting for a long time now. Good. Don't bend over anymore, squat instead—another yoga of daily living benefit. Squat when you take a shit.

Adjust your spine [4], with great respect and tenderness for the central Mt. Meru of your being. Trust your head to your hands and twist carefully. Probably you will release more tension in the form of crackling sounds. Exhale and relax as you turn your head.

This is a point of transition. The next posture is the standing posture. Rise from the squat in slow movements, the reversed folding to squat with coordinated breath, i.e. inhaling with the beginning unfolding movement, then exhaling at the all-fours-dangling-uterus movement. The inhalation as you stack each vertebra, one-by-one around your spinal column movement is a good solid transitional movement. However, you can make up your own—something that makes you feel centered and ready for the next posture.

Standing Kundalini Shakti

You will entice the kundalini with the movement of this posture and this requires the seductive sniff breath. You are now *shakti*—the female principle of life whose essence is verifiable experience of definite states of consciousness. With each staccato-sustained "sniff"-inhalation through your nostrils in an allegro rhythm, progressively contract your thighs, your ass muscles your pelvic floor or spirit muscles (pubococcygeal or Kegel muscles—the muscle that originates at your pubic bone and attaches at your coccyx or tailbone). It has three holes in it surrounded by sphincters or leavator muscles. The female bottom manifests another trinity found throughout our cosmos: the yin, yang and Tao—God the Gather, God the Son, and God the Holy Ghost; $E = MC^2$; Vishnu, Shiva and Brahma; the urethra, the anus, and the vagina. The vagina has two sets of muscles, a sphincter to open and close the entrance and a leavator to relax the passage itself in an upward and down movement. The

Aswini-mudra is the "spirit" posture of the Micronesian women, that is contracting all the muscles of the vagina while exhaling and relaxing while inhaling. This can be done anytime—no one will know that you are doing it. In pregnancy and after childbirth, this mudra is recommended 100 times a day. This will prepare you for conscious participation in birth and prevent tearing. It will help you regain tonus afterwards as well. Women in the Micronesian culture do this posture daily and call it their "spirit". When sniffing and progressively tightening thigh, ass, pelvic floor and abdominal muscles, you are coaxing the Kundalini or serpent power to arise from the womb of the shakti up your spinal column toward blissfulness. After you've inhaled as much air as you can comfortably hold without tensing any other part of your body such as feet or face or fingers or neck, you exhale and release all your tension. Then focus on the complete sense of relaxation in your thighs, ass, pelvic floor, and abdomen. This sensation is as important as the toning up movement preceding it. This is the balancing mudra and a requisite for bliss. Repeat several times the sniffing/contracting and exhaling/relaxing—feel the rhythm of this life cycle. This posture helps you contact how to release tension in the birthing area, in this way allowing you to become birth's partner.

Inner Thigh Stretch

Become a fencer in the game of living here and now. [1] Place one foot about two feet away from the other at a right angle and then slowly while exhaling, bend sideways. Keep the other leg straight and [2] you

1

2

will feel your inner thigh stretch. These muscles, ligaments, need suppleness so that you may enjoy the pleasure of pushing your baby out without tearing or bruising during the effort. Inhale as you straighten the bent leg and [3] pivot to change directions, giving the other inner thigh a [4] good stretch. You may widen your stance for more and more of a stretch and balance, and centering ability. Alternate again and again remembering to exhale as you bend and inhale as you straighten up and pivot. By the sixth time you will feel like an adept fencer taking a deep lunge. Let your arms hang freely and have your breath come easily with no stops in between the inhalation and exhalation. Focus on the moment in between inhalation and exhalation. Be aware—don't change it.

3

4

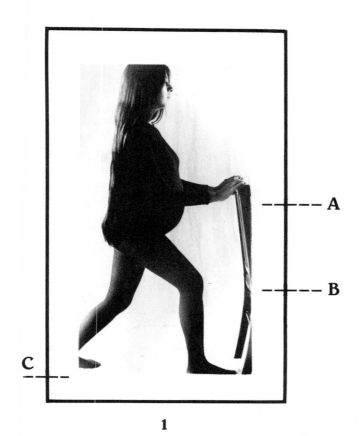

A

B

C

1

2

Lunges

A very strong and powerful posture, decep-
tively simple looking—a joy when properly
experienced. First, place your hands palm
down on a steady surface like the back of
a chair [A], on a waist-level bureau, on a
fence or, if in the woods, around the waist
of a tree. One foot will go very close to
whatever it is you are touching and the other
will go back parallel behind you with that
leg straight and the foot flat on the ground
[C]. The knee closest to the support will
bend over the foot and this angle will remain
constant throughout the entire movement
[B]. Upon conscious exhalation, the straight
leg bends [2] until the knee touches the
floor [3] whereupon you begin inhaling
through your nose and straightening the leg
to the original [1] position. Repeat this
cycle three times. On the third time down,
remain kneeling [4] and switch bent legs
[5] so that you begin inhaling coming up
[6] on the other leg, exhaling through your
mouth to a deep lunge. After three times
on this leg, stay down and slowly fold into
the next posture [7].

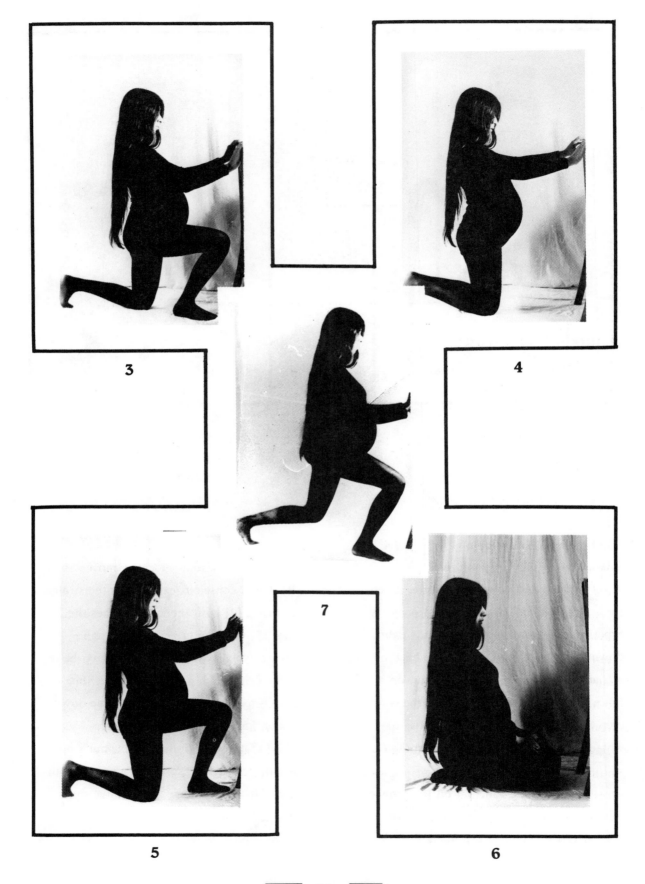

3

4

7

5

6

Thunderbolt Posture
or Sit-on-Heels

As you finish the lunges and remain kneeling, you may feel the bolt of lightning pass through the top of your head down your spine to your coccyx (tailbone). Meditate either on the thunderbolt, or on a mantra ("I am Grace of god", or whatever), or nothing—just stay sitting for a while allowing the benefits to manifest in your legs and spread throughout your being. This would be a good time to meditate for a while in whatever form you practice. If you do not already meditate, you may begin like this: keep your eyes open, focused but not staring, calm, thinking nothing, doing nothing, just sitting, aware, each moment. Women talk of their childbirth experiences being transcendent, mystical and/or the most profound spiritual experience of their lives. My hunch is that their brain rhythms were at one with the pulse of our ionosphere. Or, in other words, they were into the

"alpha" rhythm of meditation rather than the "beta" rhythm of thinking. Quiet your thoughts and sit however long you do— however long you can encounter yourself, listening to your mind chatter, letting your fantasies go without entertaining them. Let them go, be still, *be*. Bring to a close your meditation with a ritual—one in which you give yourself totally and which contains meaning in your life. My ritual is bringing my hands together, palms flat and cleaving to one another so that God may hold my hands in Hers. I then touch my fingertips to my lips, forehead and lips and back to my heart chakra. Develop one that flows for you and close each meditation the same way. It is much like when in labor greeting contractions anew with a cleansing breath— you gain strength and nourishment from the conscious repetition of meaningful movement.

An optional Tantra meditation that
gets us very, very high is:

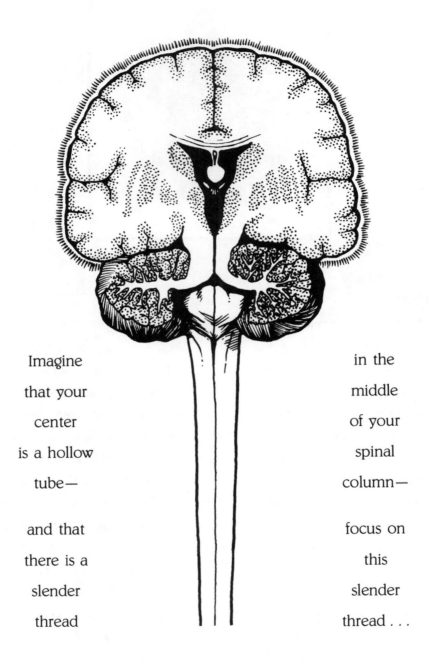

Imagine
that your
center
is a hollow
tube—

and that
there is a
slender
thread

in the
middle
of your
spinal
column—

focus on
this
slender
thread . . .

Feel the top of your head being drawn
higher—lengthening your whole spine.
Unfold your petals. With your hands lying
quietly on your thighs raise them to the
top of your head and settle into this.

Pendulum-Diaphragm Stretch

Focus on your breathing, your rhythms, the sound of your own particular "hum" (ajapna mantram) and then begin slowly bending over at your waist while exhaling to one side. Keep your vertebrae centered one over the other, allowing your spine to bend lithely like the willow, a branch in the wind of your breath. When you have bent over as far as your breath will allow, beginnings of an inspiration draw up your upper body almost effortlessly, majestically. And at apex, the momentum pushes you over—exhaling, bending to your other side. This posture is continually moving from side to side like the windshield wipers of our chevy pick-up truck. Your breath will always maintain a flow, describing a circle. It helps to think of a circle and you will find less jerky transitions between breaths. This posture benefits your diaphragm (next to your uterus the most important muscle for giving birth), your psoas muscle to give a growing trunk grace and fluidity, and your Cooper's ligaments, notorious for the "cooper's droop" of saggy tits.

1   **2**

Mountain Pose

So named because it takes as much energy to do this right as to climb a mountain. Begin by inhaling and stretching your arms above your head, turning your palms (fingers still clasped) upward (praying here for energy [1] is a possibility). Give a good stretch here to your arms and shoulders by not lifting them higher than you normally carry your shoulders. Arch your back also by allowing the pelvis to rock forward—as if someone were drawing away a string attached to your navel. Then exhaling, bring your hands back slowly to the top of your head palms down and as you almost complete this movement, your pelvis will rock, rotating toward your face. This is a contractive movement which will in turn cause your exhalation to be fuller. You will [2] use your upper thigh muscles slightly to lift you up ever so subtly, just enough to clear your ass over your heels. Repeat the cycle only three times and in subsequent practices, you may gradually increase the number of breath cycles. I have never done more than six at one time. Before you even use your thigh muscles to lift (unless you climb mountains every day, in which case ignore this), learn to coordinate the hands and breath, then hands, breath and pelvis-rocking, and finally the legs. Immediately after your last exhalation, drop to the ground on hands and knees. You are now flowing into the next posture.

Cat Stretch
or Pelvic Rocks

This posture is especially beneficial for pregnancy. Next to making love, this posture will give you preparation for experiencing intense bodily sensations and learning how to flow with contractions with a truly fluid spine. Become felinely sensual now— if out in the sunshine, feel sultry. Consciously arch your back to bring the top of your head to the tip of your spine. Actually try to bring both ends together—be the benzene ring, the snake about to swallow itself, the bow-(like in Hatha). All the while, inhale and then, feeling the movement of a circle, continue this mandala movement by exhaling long and slow and reversing your arch to be the Halloween cat, humped up. Then begin your slow inhalation and bring your belly down closer to the ground while your long neck supports a head reaching for the end of your spine in this new direction. Continue this cycle rhythmically for as long as the spirit moves you.

Dog Tail Wag

The purpose of these hand knees postures
is to give you fluidity in your trunk—this
area will be supplely toned to support your
growing uterus and allow a flowing birth
of your baby. Now that you have stretched
your trunk lengthwise in the Cat Stretch,
you will stretch sideways. This is very much
like the diaphragm stretch on another level.
Pretend you are a dog wagging its tail. This
is the basic movement. Your head will reach
around toward your ass, keeping your trunk
parallel to the floor. Make a big bend that
will make you conscious of your waist.
This is one of the few things you can do at
the end of your pregnancy which will let
you feel like you *do* have a waistline. The
breath is the same as Diaphragm Stretch—
exhale as you bend and inhale as you arc
over to the other side. Take care that you
don't bend your knees to either side as you
exhale—all the movement is in the trunk.

The Python

Holding energy in your trunk will work against yourself and your baby. Lots of these energy blocks can be made conscious in the next posture. Remember how pythons gracefully ingest whole animals and through peristalsis swallow them? The movement is snake-like and very sensual in a circular motion. Begin by arching your back—like you were about to do the cat hump, only do not bring your head up. Your head will remain relaxed at the neck, either hanging gently, loosly down or parallel to the floor.

Instead your back will slowly circle to the left and continue the revolution to the opposite posture of the cat stretch with your belly closest to the floor. Continue the smooth circular motion to the right now and so on till you feel your trunk going smoothly round and round. If for a moment you do not try any special breathing, your breath will eventually settle into the most natural pattern and rhythm for this round-the-world posture. Do these circles in both directions.

The Centaur

The breath for this posture is natural though a little slower than usual. One leg extends behind you directly as far as your pelvic ligaments will allow. You'll probably feel a delicious stimulation to the corresponding buttock. The hands are moved up and down along an imaginary force field plane parallel to your spine to that special place of effortless balance. Once you find this space, relax into it with your breath. Then switch to the other side. This posture feels especially aquarian to me despite the ancient name of centaur. I showed the posture to my daughter asking what it reminded her of and she gave it the name we now use, the centaur. Pay attention to your two internal flowers, your ovaries. This posture will energize them.

1

2

3

In Preparation for The Next Postures

Pictured are the best ways to get down onto your back [1,2,3] and conversely the way to get up again without straining abdominal muscles.

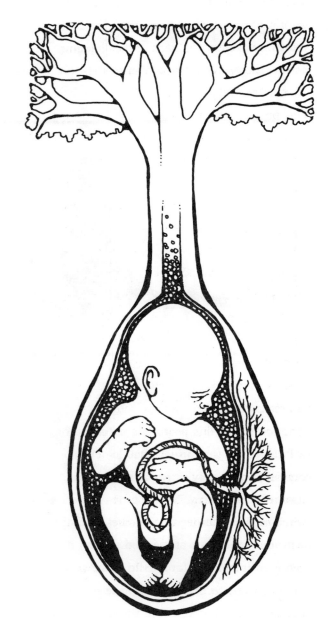

Pelvis Leg Lifts

For a while, focus on this new level of being supine. Feel where the ground supports you, where your body makes contact with the floor—your head, back, ass, thighs, calves, heels. Likewise, feel the spaces between the ground and your body—the back of your neck, the small of your back, maybe the back of your knees. If your sacrum bothers you in this posture, place the hands palms down under your buttocks and this should take the pressure off the small of your back. This posture endears itself to me for bringing my awareness to the here-now. If I am not exactly centered in this posture continually, I will goof up. This is due to the breath and movement coordination which at first seems highly unnatural but really isn't. Again, when you bring limbs closer to your body you exhale, and so you begin by taking a deep, conscious inhalation at rest and upon the exhalation you lift your leg *using the muscles in your pelvis*. Use your breath to raise your leg by directing it to your pelvis—your thigh muscles should be relatively released. When you reach the natural end of your exhalation, you inhale allowing your leg to easily float down to the floor. Here you rest a complete breath cycle, that is another exhalation first then inhalation, and then you switch to the other leg and let the exhalation raise your other leg with your toes *not* pointed (the pointing à la ballet may cause you a calf muscle cramp) and feel how long your leg is and how it connects deep inside

your pelvis. Upon inhalation, lower your leg, rest for the complete breath cycle before changing legs and lift the other leg. Repeat approximately six times taking care not to strain your legs. If your legs shake, you are lifting them too high.

Pelvic Rock Abdomen

Lying on your back, draw your knees up allowing them to spread naturally as though you were welcoming your lover. The motion will be the rocking of your pelvis, like Cat Stretch but on a new level. Be aware especially of your abdominal muscles and your neck muscles and the little bones that make up your lowest spine, the sacrum and the coccyx or tailbone. You may actually feel each articulation of the tail bones if this posture is done slowly enough and you are blessed without any energy blocks here. On the inhalation, ready yourself by totally releasing your spine into the floor. Then exhale, slowly, consciously and press your lower back into the floor, bringing your head up to look in between your legs [1]. Keep your shoulders grounded and be gentle on your abdomen and neck. Hold till you feel the need for oxygen and then upon inhalation, rock the other way, arching your back—leaving a tunnel between your lower back and the floor—to the extent that you could slip your arm all the way through [2]. Repeat so that your lower back once again presses against the floor and your head is up—this motion can be done vertebra by vertebra. If you like, you may pause here to give your abdominal muscles extra tonus,

1

but please do not become athletic about it for this will cause strain. Continue this cycle for as long as it feels right—attending to your even breath and the releasing of neck, abdomen and lower back. This posture is reported to cure chronic backaches in pregnancy and prevent back labor also if done religiously, within or without the yoga routine.

At this point you may insert your favorite Hatha or Kundalini postures as long as they feel comfortable. Yoga and even Tai Chi Chuan are often prohibited to pregnant persons out of a fear place. I've been told, for example, that inverted postures are

2

downright dangerous. My feeling is if you are in touch with yourself, you will be able to feel if certain postures are the wrong kind of energy to invite into your pregnant being. Pay close attention to messages from your womb—especially from the top of your uterus, the fundus. This is where your placenta is situated, most likely. If you feel at all cramped here, delete that particular posture from your practice—a squished placental bed will cut off vital nutrients to your baby as long as you hold the posture. Adepts may inadvertently interfere with their babies' life supplies for minutes at a time. The few postures pictured here were my favorites up until my eighth lunar month of pregnancy wherein the half shoulderstand [1] became uncomfortable and so I gave it up and to keep in balance, deleted the fish posture [2] also. Again, let me repeat one thought about the "non-prenatal yoga" postures: only do the ones you feel at home with, probably the postures you have practiced in your pre-pregnant era of this lifetime and to which you are especially attached.

1

2

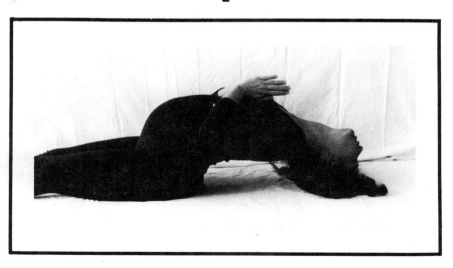

1

2

The Hiss Breath

Try to become a snake, a muscular peristaltic beholder of great secrets—you are coiled, sitting on your heels, wide open beaver, and inhaling deeply [1]. Eyes flickering like the tongue-sensor of the snake, you drop your head slowly, deliberately, one vertebra at a time, kind of like Folding To Squat [2]. As your head moves to the floor, a hiss comes from the corners of your mouth and this sound fills your spine, your whole head and brain. Your arms are placed to your sides, palms up behind you. They remain released. Your forehead leads you down and once you contact the floor, you turn your head to either side. Shoulders and arms fall naturally to the side and here you stay, snake-warm and languid [3]. On any inhalation you choose begin to turn your head from cheek resting place to forehead readiness. Slowly reverse the motion down, again coming up one vertebra at a time, no hissing.

3

1

2

Camel

This is the complement to the Hiss Breath and sometimes it feels best to engage the two postures in an intercourse of motion, first always the Hiss down and up and then the flow to the Camel (called Camel because of the "hump" which is your enlarging uterus). Imagining myself a camel, the ship of the desert, I can feel the motion of sand-waves and my serene cruise to the oasis. I am in the oasis and drinking in the life-supporting cool air. Rest on your hands behind you with your legs still open as in the Hiss Breath [1]. Drop your head back-wards slowly and allow your trunk to float towards the sky, higher and higher, your

arms supporting. At the crest of this move-ment you can feel all the muscles in your bottom stretch down to your thighs and feel the strengthening of your lower back and upper arms [2]. Now you exhale as you lower yourself down to the sitting on heels resting posture [1]. And then you are ready to inhale again and then hiss down as the snake or do another camel as the spirit moves you. These two postures repeated again and again are a mantra for your body, a dance which will be your last gross movements before you quiet and still yourself for subtle breath and relaxation, the two pillars of yoga practice and childbirth preparation.

Breath

Two breathing patterns are included here
though you may at this point add others
that especially are meaningful for you.
These breath postures will benefit your
preparation for natural childbirth whether
the method you plan to use is Lamaze,
Pavlov-Lamaze, Jacobsen, Bradley or
Kitzinger, or any combination, synthesis
or new creation you may come up with.
The importance here is the consciousness
with which you approach breath training.
For years I have been instructing my natural
childbirth students to feel their breath as
a circular flow and image consciously a
circle as they breathed. I understand that
waves in the ocean are made up of water
molecules moving in ellipses (and a circle
is a special kind of ellipse). The energy of

the wave moves freely through these elliptical motions and yet the integrity of the molecular bodies is always intact. This is how childbirth will be for you—an energy coming through you in which your center, your breath, will always remain in motion and yet retain its integrity. Childbirth and the necessary tidings of your womb have often been likened to the waves of the ocean. You use your breath not to distract you from the oceanic experience but to keep from "drowning", i.e. running out of oxygen and causing yourself needless pain.

You may do these breath postures in any body mudra at any time; however, at the end of a prenatal yoga series, lie on your back with your legs drawn up, knees falling open and ankles crossed, or feet on the floor by your sides. Labels such as abdominal breathing or diaphragmatic breathing are inappropriate here—your whole being is breathing now. Place your hands on your center, with openness between your fingers and thumb forming the symbol of wholeness. As you breathe deeply, follow the path of the air, feel it enter through your nostrils, windpipe, bronchioles and lungs and now some magic —the breath continues through your diaphragm into your abdominal cavity to immerse your whole uterus and pelvis in oxygen. As you exhale, imagine a faucet in your navel that allows tension to leave your self with the exhalation continuing through your diaphragm, lungs, bronchioles, windpipe and mouth. Do this for a while, trip on it. Imagine that the air you breathe

is golden colored light and bathe your insides with this light energy. The next step is to expand the magic—as you bring your breath into your abdominal cavity, feel it bathe your digestive, urinary and sexual organs. Let this feeling spread to your external genital organs and especially feel your vagina fill with your breath. Then send this sensation down into your thighs, legs, all the way to your feet. Exhale and bring your breath back like the wind. Continue this cyclical process until you are lost in it.

Puff Breath

Dragon-like, ballon-fish like, inhale through your nose short, smooth breaths to fill up your abdomen—so much as to actually raise your belly over your womb. You'll be lifting your abdominal wall off your uterus in effect. When you reach the limit of inhalations, exhale through your mouth slowly and be aware of the moment when your belly touches your uterus again. The value of this in childbirth would be a decrease in discomfort you may feel caused by a heavy belly on a sensitive uterus, for a womb in labor interprets heavy pressure as a pain stimulus.

Moon-Sun Breath

The left nostril is your moon (ida) and the right your sun (pingala). In Tantric Yoga there is this idea that at the moment of the woman's orgasm, if she is breathing through the right nostril, the baby conceived from that union will be a boy. When I was crazy last spring, and trying to conceive a baby boy (using the ovulation method and astrological sex selection and bio-rhythms), each attempt brought my finger to my left nostril to plug it up. I never felt so silly being plugged in my whole life. Eventually I gave up this ego involvement in the selection of our second baby's sex. (Besides, I can't decide which I'd rather have now anyway. I was inculcated with the notion that the first baby "should" be a boy and so our daughter has especially been a great teacher in freeing me from this bit of cultural programming.)

For Moon-Sun Breath, your breath will continue to flow in a circle, no breaks in between the inhalation and exhalation but you will consciously direct breath in one nostril and out the other. Begin by placing your finger on your left nostril and inhale thorugh your right nostril—then switch and exhale through your left nostril. Inhale through the same (the left) and then switch to plug up your left nostril and exhale through yur right, switch, etc. Each time you exhale you switch nostrils and then continue to inhale through the same nostril. The fingers are held up to energize the 72,000 nerve-like pathways of your subtle body—they act like antennae. This is especially helpful in bringing clarity to your self—I sometimes do it when feeling muddled or muddy, or before I write or during reading of difficult material. I can imagine the oxygen nourishing my brain easily as I breathe Moon-Sun.

Progressive Relaxation

This is the final posture to prenatal yoga and very important in a ritualistic sense. This posture brings closure to your daily practice and from this ritual you will gain a sense of meaning. While in the Progressive Relaxation posture, you reap the benefits of all the preceding postures. A great feeling of serenity will envelop you, a feeling of fulfilling your own dharma. The chant you will learn is the same we use in labor coaching—accompanied by massage and energy from our heart chakras. I use this chant every evening before sleep and before naps also and have yet to experience "insomnia", even when traveling through my heaviest crises and changes. You will need to lie down, very comfortably, using pillows if necessary to achieve this and in a warm, quiet space. This posture should be maintained at least fifteen minutes. Chant very slowly, savoring the release of tensions and worries. If you lie on your back, you may find the pressure on your tailbone (during the latter months of pregnancy) relieved by crossing your ankles. This isn't highly recommended though—your body relaxes easier when you're open. My favorite posture is the "running" posture, lying on my abdomen with one knee drawn up and my head turned in the direction of my drawn up leg (also known as the tonic neck reflex of newborn infants). Once settled, begin by focusing on your breath and by just watching your self—how are you now? How do you greet your breath, where do you send it, or block it, or does your breath *do you?* Imagine that you are now a candle in the hot sun, melting slowly into the floor. Feel your body growing heavier, so heavy that you sink into the floor, through the ground, to the center of the earth . . . and on. Feel gravity push on you and your pushing on gravity. Feel your shoulders opening, your shoulder blades spreading— your pelvis opening, spreading wider, looser. Your arms and legs are totally limp. Imagine that you are a sandbag and that the sand is slowly leaking out through your fingertips and your toes . . . or through the back of

your head, from behind your ears. When you are quiet, peaceful, begin this chant (chant silently to yourself): I am relaxing my feet, my feet are releasing, I am relaxing my feet . . . I am relaxing my ankles, my ankles are releasing, I am relaxing my ankles . . . I am releasing my calves, my shins are relaxing, I am relaxing my lower legs . . . I am relaxing my knees, my knees are releasing, I am relaxing my knees . . . I am relaxing my thighs, my upper legs are relaxing, I am releasing my thighs . . . I am relaxing my pelvic floor, my pelvic floor is releasing, I am relaxing my pelvic floor . . . I am relaxing my ass, my ass is relaxing, I am releasing my ass . . . I am relaxing my lower back, my tailbone and sacrum are releasing, I am relaxing my lower back . . . I am relaxing my middle back, my lumbar spine is relaxing, I am releasing my back, I am relaxing my upper back, my thoracic and cervical vertebrae are relaxing, I am relaxing my upper back . . . I am releasing my neck, my neck is relaxing, I am relaxing my neck . . . I am releasing my head, I am releasing my head, my forehead is relaxing, I am relaxing my eyebrows, the muscles around my eyes are relaxing, I am releasing my eyelids (feel the relaxation spread from my eyelids deep into my being), I am relaxing my eyeballs, my nose is releasing, the muscles around my nose are relaxing, I am relaxing my cheeks, my ears are releasing, the muscles around my ears are relaxing, I am relaxing my jaws, my mouth is hanging limply open, I am relaxing my mouth, the back of my tongue is releasing, my lips are relaxing, I am relaxing my chin, I am releasing my throat, I feel the relaxation spread down into my shoulders, I am relaxing my shoulders, my shoulders are releasing, I am relaxing my shoulders . . . I am releasing my upper arms, my upper arms are relaxing, I am relaxing my upper arms . . . I am releasing my elbows, my elbows are relaxing, I am relaxing my elbows . . . my lower arms are relaxing, I am releasing my forearms, I am relaxing my lower arms . . . I am relaxing my wrists, my wrists are releasing, I am relaxing my wrists . . . my hands are relaxing, my hands are relaxing, I am releasing my hands . . . (feel the relaxation spread to my fingertips), I am relaxing my chest, I am relaxing my chest, my breasts are relaxing . . . I am relaxing my abdomen, my belly is relaxing, my belly is releasing . . . I am relaxing my pelvis, my pelvis is relaxing . . . I am releasing my pelvis . . . I am relaxing

my internal organs, my internal organs are relaxing, I am releasing my lungs, my heart is releasing, I am relaxing my circulatory systems, I am releasing my stomach, my intestines are relaxing, I am relaxing my liver, my pancreas, my spleen, my gall bladder, my digestive organs are completely released, I am relaxing my kidneys, my bladder is relaxing, my lower intestine and rectum are relaxing, my excretory system is completely relaxed, I am relaxing my uterus, my ovaries are releasing, I am relaxing my vagina, my sexual organs are releasing and completely relaxed, I am relaxing my skin, my skin is glowingly alive, I am releasing my skin, I am relaxing my brain, I am relaxing my brain, I am relaxing my brain . . . I am relaxing my whole body, I am relaxing my whole being, I am releasing my entire self, I am totally relaxed.

Now focus on how it feels to be
relaxed and alert at the same time . . .

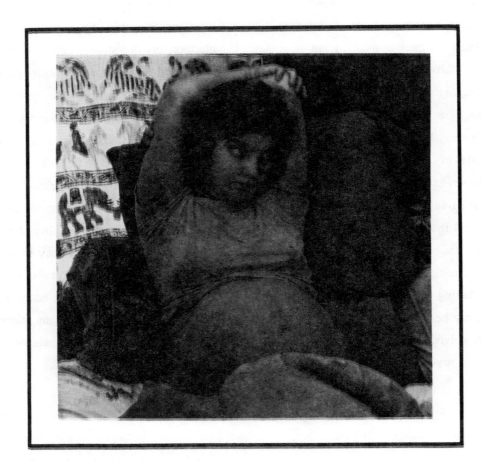

In memory of Beth, who shared her natural childbirth experience
with me. It was the first for both of us and I am eternally grateful.
Through knowing this sister, my teachings became alive and I truly
realized the responsibilities of life and death karma.
                                Jeannine Parvati Baker

emerging

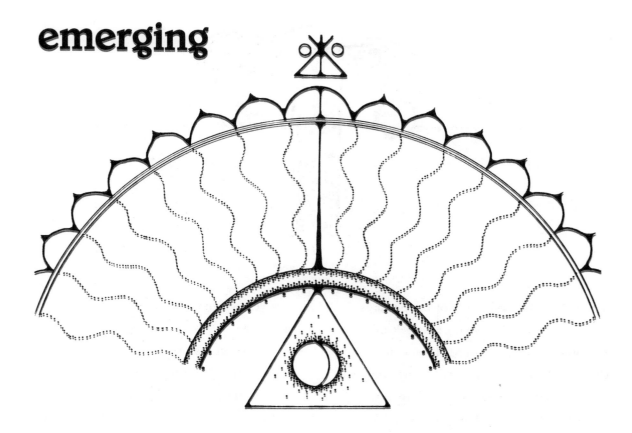

Birth Report of Loi Caitlin
first-born, January 25, 1970
female, Aquarius ☉ Virgo ☽

I woke up Saturday morning after a night of Braxton Hicks contractions and an impending intuition that soon we would be three. Experiencing difficulty in tying my boot laces for the first time, I remember mentioning to Michael that this is going to be my last day pregnant. All that day we both felt wondrously energized so we cleaned, re-roofed our goat shed, and generally did lots of stuff so that I was only subliminally conscious of breathing with my hour-or-so-apart contractions. By ten o'clock Saturday night, we had recorded the intervals between contractions and I still need not have been doing my first labor

breathing but to my inexperienced reality in regard to childbirth, contractions required some response so I did deep breathing till 11:00 p.m. when Michael called the doctor. Contractions were four minutes apart and as we had an hour drive to San Francisco, Dr. Miller advised us to come in right away. We had chosen this hospital because they would interfere the least with how we wanted to give birth. I had had no show, natural diarrhea, bags of water breaking— just regular contractions and a feeling that my baby's journey had begun. I arrived at the hospital at midnight and was made to sit in a wheelchair, which I did good-

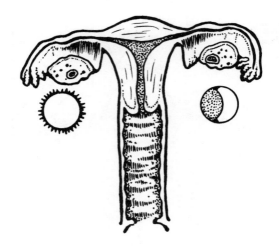

humoredly. My room was not the pastures with running brook I would have felt more comfortable in but I had Michael with whom I felt secure and calm—he was my home. He was spirited away by a receptionist to fill out even more forms and I was left alone for a while. No prep, enema, examination—all my choice, which I declined. I discovered that I remained centered and carried my own home totally within myself. I stayed lying on either side in the progressive relaxation posture of yoga or in a fetal position since we figured that after a hard day's work I'd be sleeping: I may as well still my body like sleep. Contractions became more and more compelling—"focus on me" they insisted, and I did. My uterus had taken command of my body—even my governing brain conceded to the urgency of my uterus. I was in rhythm with the cosmic flow—being a vessel for this life ritual changed my usual semi-scattered existence into one pure practice. With every contraction my breathing responded for

our very survival—OXYGEN—prana-here and now.

Michael massages, Michael chants and I am being reborn along with my baby. Five centimeters dilated (I knew before the doctor announced my progress to me) and feeling contractions getting more and more intense (really closer together and new sensations to integrate caused by the flexing of my baby's head). Having difficulty and occasional cramps cause me distress. The nurse sees my tenseness and offers me medication. Michael wisely looks into my eyes saying "You know what is best for you and I am here with you *now*." I decided not to numb myself to my own experience (I was not suffering). The nurse later became my own mother figure and her stocky reassuring presence inspired my efforts. We worked hard—accelerating fast shallow breathing for a few century seconds and decelerating together. Breathing as a prayer, our union completed with each contraction. Around eight centimeters dilation I felt a

change—transition—and I shook as the soul
entered my baby. Contractions came closer
and closer together and I threw-up, had
my bag of waters broken to a gush of warm,
watery relief and felt wonderful. There was
to be no more pain. Now I was dancing—
my body was creating through powerful
muscle movements and sensitive responsive
counter-movements my unique art form:
labor as mudra: meditative movement.
Exhilarated, I felt the urge to push, quite
a pleasurable sensation and began pushing
on the labor bed. In the delivery room,
I squatted on the table to the delight of
all the attendants and gave myself to
pushing.

What primal pleasure to push—each
cell, atom pushing aware of every second,
every sensation. I lay back slightly from
my squatting posture to allow Dr. Miller

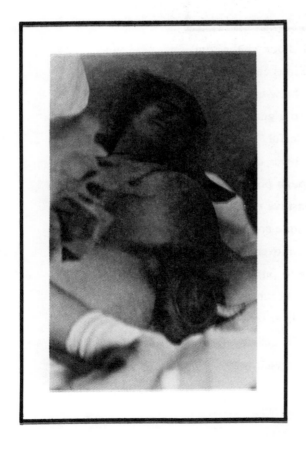

access for support of my baby's now crown=
ing head. I'm immersed in the moment which
is more than time—more than a fourth
dimension of our reality—all my soul has
been and will be is revealed to me now and
then Loi's head emerges fully and she opens
her eyes and our eyes lock. I feel another
being so wise teach me more in the eye=
locked moment than in the whole twenty
years of my life. Another contraction and
I push out her shoulders, the rest of Loi's
body flows out and with it a great sensation
of release, total release and she (for now I
see her sex—and am grateful for seeing
myself—with great respect Michael and
Dr. Miller allowed this revelation to come
directly from my daughter to me) she
begins to cry, and I begin to cry with joy
and Michael cries and we share our con=
scious blessing and Dr. Miller and the nurse
are crying too. Loi is handed to me still
attached to our placenta via umbilical cord
and we say, "Loi Caitlin, welcome—ah baby,
baby, our baby." She quiets and with her

big wise eyes greets her parents. Sunday
morning, 6:58, at dawn; San Francisco
6 lbs. 18 inches. Alive.

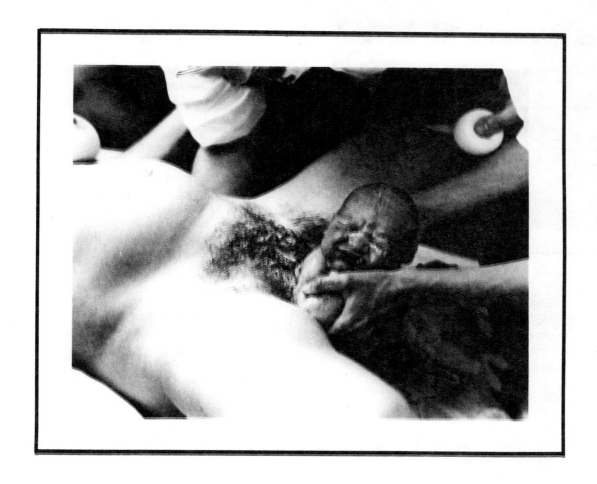

sixteen

First born
Light landed
On our Earth.
Given, delivered
and trusted to me.

Thrown deep
into love.
You showed me
one way through.
Sightless matter,
the inward eye
emerging new.

Looking at you
my mother's face
slipping down,
an old bathrobe
fallen to feet
as we enter
the waters together.

Sins of self
washing away,
we come clean
before the judge
sentenced to cult
and bond forever.

Now you are sixteen
and never been kissed
by the otherknown or
bound to the standing wave
of his love,
invited to look
again at beginnings.

This is one of those.
Beginnings, the fresh
glance into creation.
Woman my daughter is
as I see my own death
come closer.
She catches hold of life
in our relay race
of generation.

Time marks me
her daughter, a crone.
Running still we shared
too much. A body,
two souls.
When I finish
let me toss to you
eternity.
Carry it true.

Jeannine Parvati Baker
30 January 86
Joseph, Utah

emerging

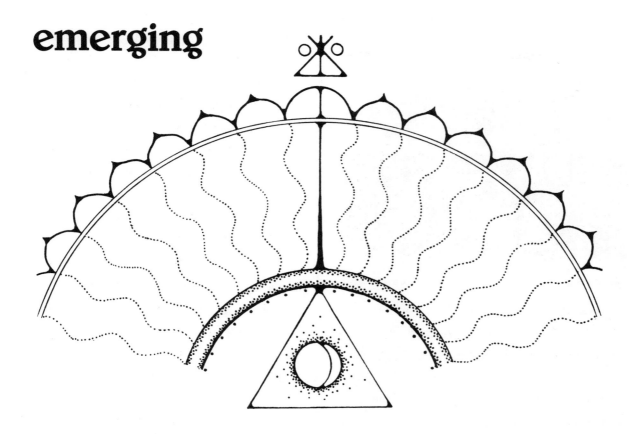

**Birth Report of Oceana Violet and Cheyenne
Coral second and third born, August 2, 1974
females, Leo ☉, Aquarius ☽**

Walking Out of the Hospital

This is the birth which made me a midwife.
I imagine that only dying to the self could be
as strong a testimony to the spirit as birth is.

In part I became a midwife in response
to this birth experience of my twins, my
second pregnancy. Up til then I was a friend,
a labor-coach or monitrice at births. I was
fascinated by birth and devoted to helping
my sisters give birth in joy, peace, trust—and
with their families bonding in love.

Being pregnant with my twins provided
an opportunity to learn all I could. Especially
as we expected no one would help us have
a home birth. Because of my twins I was
labelled "high-risk", even though I knew full
well that they would deliver just perfectly.
My health was optimum and there was a lot
of love in my life. Yet, I was a "category",
not a unique person anymore, and it was difficult to gain medical help. At the time of
this pregnancy, there were few professionals
who would risk attending a home birth of
twins. This was the year *Prenatal Yoga* was
first published.

One of my twins was in a breech position, a "high-risk" condition in itself.

"Walking Out of the Hospital," first
published in *Birth Stories: The Experience
Remembered*, edited by Janet Isaacs Ashford

Especially so when coming first before a head-down twin. It was feared that their chins might lock, impeding birth. Actually, an obstetrician friend of mine called me one morning while I was eating breakfast hot-cakes to tell me that if I delivered the breech first and their chins locked, he might have to decapitate them both to deliver them without killing me!

However I knew in my heart that my babies and I stood a safer chance at home with trusted friends, than with paranoid professionals educated way beyond their intelligence.

In fact, I resolved to trust Heavenly Mother (or whomever was on call the night I birthed my twins) and let go of reliance on anyone other than myself, the babies, and Her to give birth.

As it was in the early 1970's, there was not much support for unattended home births. I was more interested in doing what was best for my twins than in "setting trends" and so rather than try to persuade medical professionals to attend, I asked some close friends to help me deliver. We had meetings weekly before the birth. We all spoke our fears, desires and affirmations for a peaceful delivery. I delegated tasks to my friends so that the father of our babies and I could spend those first few precious moments just being with our babies. We all meditated as a group and grew in trust of one another.

I feel it was the nature of my twins as much as our need as parents which brought together that friendship circle. The twins are remarkable for bringing people into my life and they began right away. Some wise voice within guided me to extend myself to others preparing for their births. From the start my pregnancy seemed to be less for me personally and more for our community. I felt a shift from experiencing myself alone to being with others and caring about others passionately in a way unknown before. I was alone-among-others and still felt one hundred percent responsible for my own birth. I TRUSTED THAT THE COMING BIRTH WOULD HAPPEN THE WAY IT WAS MEANT TO BE.

The night I went into labor, my hus-band said to me, "Let's go to the movies, because soon the babies will be here and we won't be able to go out together again for awhile." I knew the babies were very close to coming, but since my husband rarely ask-ed me for a date, I accepted. We saw "The Three Musketeers" and as I already felt quite pulled inwards to focus on the twins, I really don't remember the movie except for all the bloodshed, which I hoped was not portentous.

I DO remember the breech baby (Oceana)

kicking my cervix, like peddling a bicycle, during the film! After the movie we came home and my husband fell asleep. Our four and one half year old daughter Loi slept by us. I stayed up and practiced my prenatal yoga as I had never done before. My flexibility and concentration were at their best. As I retired, I whispered to my sleeping family that tonight the babes would be born. I was happy.

I awoke probably less than an hour later in a puddle of liquid. "Funny," I thought, "to begin labor with my bag of waters breaking." I got up and sloshed my way into the bathroom and then filled up the toilet bowl with more amniotic fluid, or so I thought. What a shock, when I turned on the light to see the bowl filled with blood! More was gushing from me and I stuffed a towel

between my legs and waddled back to the bedroom. Turning on the light brought a gruesome sight—there was blood everywhere, from the bed all along our white wall-to-wall carpet to the toilet, and now the towel I was wearing was soaked with blood also. "That movie!" I thought, "Now there's blood all over the place!" I woke up my husband and we decided it would be best to get medical help, as this wasn't something he felt he could handle alone.

I had previously had a suspicion that my placenta might be marginally placed over my cervix. In fact, I had agreed to take the long drive the next morning to San Francisco for a sonogram test, which could show where the placenta was situated. I had prayed my labor would begin before that grueling drive and the medical test. Now it had, but I was bleeding more than I had ever seen or heard of as normal.

I called an obstetrician friend of mine, who agreed to meet me at the local hospital. We called a neighbor to come sit with our Loi. As I left the house, my neighbor stuffed into my pocket some herbs to stop the bleeding.

We were admitted at about 2:00 A.M. with no contractions yet begun. I was bleeding enough to have soaked another bath towel by that time. However, despite the bleeding, I did not feel weak. I felt a lot of love for all the people I met at the hospital. Even the coldness of the sterile conditions didn't bother me. I asked the nurse to check me and see if my placenta was the cause of the bleeding but she said she couldn't do anything like that as such examination and diagnosis are the doctor's province. I had to submit to a battery of tests before the doctor would even come.

Meanwhile I had been drinking lots of bayberry bark and shepherd's purse tea—the herbs given to me by my neighbor. A cup of hot water was the only thing I asked of the hospital. I steeped the herbs in the water and after I drank a cupful or two, the bleeding subsided. I was feeling great and contractions began slowly, rapidly gaining strength. They were completely painless if I concentrated and surrendered to them. My breech baby was still riding high and did not apply painful pressure on my cervix. I spent three hours dilating and I could feel I was entering transition even before the doctor arrived to check me out.

But instead of my obstetrician friend, in walked his partner, the same doctor who had called me during breakfast with the image of decapitating babies' heads. When I asked where my firend was, the partner said it was his turn for night duty. I told him a special agreement had been made between myself and my doctor friend, yet he was adamant that it was his turn! I burst into tears. This was another "sign of transition," and also, as I have been realizing lately, a deep purification. I cried out my disappointment. I was very attached to the idea of my friend meeting me at the hospital if need be, as his attitude was very supportive for breech delivery and I knew that not many other doctors felt comfortable in delivering bottom-first babies, whether at home or in the hospital. But I stopped crying. My trust and faith returned, knowing that this doctor standing in front of me would do his best too.

He examined me and said the placenta was fine. I asked him why the copious blood flow had happened and he said he didn't know. I felt I could now carry on without worrying about my placenta. I had been visualizing the placenta migrating away from the opening of my cervix steadily for three hours and that coupled with my herbal teas to stop hemorrhage, was all that was done to help me.

At that point I asked the doctor if a vaginal birth was possible. He ordered an X-ray, which I didn't want. I had been X-rayed as a fetus during my mother's labor and have always had that extra fear of radiation exposure. This was a fear I didn't want to

pass on to my children.

However, the doctor insisted and, because I also wanted information, I yielded. This is my only regret in the story. I was wheeled into the X-ray room and I concentrated on surrounding myself in white light to protect my babies from the radiation. After the X-ray, the technician took a long time to come out of his lead-walled room, so I got off the gurney and walked back into the labor room. Back in the labor bed, I heard a flurry all along the hallway—"Where is she? She has disappeared!" Finally I realized they were talking about me! No one had ever seen a woman in transition with twins walk back!

Some time after the twins' birth, I asked for a copy of those X-rays and a doctor told me that there was no way the hip bones of the woman pictured could vaginally deliver those babies. He would have C-sectioned the parturient! Luckily the doctor who was helping me in labor read the X-rays differently. He said a vaginal delivery was possible. So I seized the moment and asked if our daughter Loi could come to the labor room and watch the births of her siblings. "No way, it's against all hospital policy" was the answer. I was very close to full dilation at this point and feeling a little spaced-out. Yet the vision of my family being together at the birth was strong. I then informed everyone that we would be leaving the hospital. It was more important to me to be with my daughter than to have the help of these kind professionals.

They thought I was joking. Even my husband did! Yet I was getting up and preparing to leave. To try and change my mind, the doctor said, "Mother Nature has given you a signal by all the bleeding, to stay in the hospital." I told him that I was in touch with Mother Nature and She was telling me to go home to my daughter.

Next, the doctor went into conference with my husband in the hallway and all I could hear of that conversation was my husband's testimony as to how strong-willed I am. The doctor then called several nurses as "witnesses" and made a loud statement, loud enough so that I could hear, that the patient was leaving against his better medical judgement. He brought in a paper for me to sign, which basically said that I relieved the doctor and hospital of all blame if I died as a result of leaving the hospital. I signed it eagerly. In a last heroic try, the doctor placed his arms in the door on either side and his feet squarely at each corner of the exitway and said, "Jeannine, over my dead body will you leave!"

My reply, equally as desperate with the drama now unfolding, was, "That could be arranged, Doctor!" With that, we left.

As we walked out of the hospital, the doctor called out saying that I would drop these babies out of me before we even made it home. I could feel there was no pressure yet on my cervix and though fully dilated by now, I knew we would make it home to deliver. The doctor then said, "How long to get to your house?" both my husband and I said, "Twelve minutes."

This was a family joke. We always said "twelve" when asked for a number we really

didn't know.

"I'm going to follow you," the doctor said. I hadn't an argument left in me at that point.

We arrived home just before dawn and found that our neighbor had made up the birthing bed, lit candles and incense, and called our friends to arrive as previously planned. But try as he might, he hadn't been able to get a hold of the only midwife in our county, who had reluctantly accepted the possibility of coming if we had no one else to help. The doctor with his nurse, arrived looking sleepy. "Exactly twelve minutes!" he said, looking at his watch. He asked where the spare bedroom was and promptly fell asleep.

It felt so wonderful being home! The soft lighting was a relief after the glare of hospital and the fragrant smell of incense was more comforting than antiseptics. My daughter lay peacefully asleep next to me as I began to feel the pressure of the first twin's descent. It took a couple of hours for the

breech baby to rotate into position. The doctor awoke at one point and asked if I wanted him to turn the baby manually, helping it come out sooner. My feeling was that the baby knew best how and when to come. No thank you. My yogic breathing kept me open, soft and peaceful and I still had no pain!

As the rosy fingered dawn crept upon us, I could feel Oceana, my first born twin,

slide into my center. Now the urge to push came on strong and I roared her down my birth canal. In between my loud pushing sounds, I would say, "How wonderful! It feels so good!" If I hadn't recorded that on tape, I might even doubt it myself. This was my first painless labor and delivery; a cherished gift.

Oceana's little feet poked out of me and I reached around, in my hands and

knees position, to feel her warm and kicking. Pushing out a breech baby was very different from the vertex (head first) delivery I had experienced four and one half years before. Loi woke up, not during my roaring, but just when Oceana was delivering. Loi integrated remarkably well what was happening—the room was filled with people, there was a foot of her sister sticking out of her mother, and she took all this in her stride.

During a contraction my attention would focus, as in a tunnel, on the task at hand. In between contractions I played hostess, film director, audio technician, and mother to my Loi. When the doctor asked Loi whether she would like to have a sister or a brother she replied that "either the baby is a boy or a girl." She said this very

phenomenologically and without a hint of preference.

The birth process itself taught me how to deliver a breech. Once the breech baby's head entered my birth canal, I felt I could get some traction by pushing from within through my abdominal muscles. The baby slid right out. There she lay beneath me (I was still on all fours, holding onto my husband's body for leverage) and the room filled with violet colored light. The baby was indeed quite purple. The doctor said, "There she is Jeannine; now get her going." Since I had been at births with this doctor, he knew my capability and allowed me this greatest privilege, of being the one to massage and cuddle my baby into breath. When she began her sputtering we were all quite moved and I was in bliss.

"My baby, my baby," I kept crooning over and over. There are only a few times my voice sounds like that—when having orgasms, when birthing babies, and when praying.

"We still have another one in there, don't forget," the nurse's efficient voice reminded us. And no sooner said than I felt a wave of expulsion take me over.

"Oh here it comes!" With the help of my friends I turned over to a seated pose, holding my first twin in my arms as the second one came into my birth canal. She was coming so fast! What a rush I felt and ecstasy filled me to the brim.

"Don't spurt her, don't spurt her!" The doctor's voice came through to me and I only pushed once to have her on my perineum, a gush of waters about her now crowning head. I breathed slowly and delivered her into one arm in a matter of seconds, stretching easily and painlessly. There was our Cheyenne, all pink and crying from her quick entrance. The room filled with coral colored light and I scooped her up next to her sister and held them both close to my breasts. The second twin arrived just seven minutes after the first. The sun was streaming in and it was a warm clear day.

True to my "Three Musketeers" form, I then began a postpartum hemorrhage and delivered the placenta amidst more than the usual amount of blood. The doctor said, for the last time, "Mother Nature is giving you a sign to return to the hospital." I merely asked for my herb teas, all handy now at

home, and stopped bleeding in a few minutes.

"Well, you were right once about Mother Nature," said the doctor, "so I guess I'll just have to trust you again."

What a marvelous lesson for him, to learn to trust the birthing woman as being the one who knows best what is going on!

Finally, our family learned that doctors and hospitals can be allies in the birthing process. However their services are optional and as we heal birth more in our culture, it will be easier to reclaim birth from a medical emergency, to a simple EMERGENCE.

Out Draws Beauty
By The Midwife

Out draws beauty by the midwife
called to bedside this night
She comes as two doves
or as crone her bag as light
as she is able
Psyche's midwife either flies
to a birth   or is already there
the tea, the touch, the care
receiving the christ-child
again and again and again

Jeannine Parvati Baker
First published in *Mother Poet*
by Mothering Magazine

Carry Me Earthside

Carry me earthside passion
let heaven roll over me.
Love throws me here
now caught, then free
to give birth gracefully.

Carry me earthside labor
let my midwife guide us well
through the ring of fire
the bonds of illusion
to see the one who births me.

Carry me earthside childbirth
let my love-fruit fall so gently.
Turn me inside out re-born
and at service
for my babe, my mate and Thee.

Jeannine Parvati Baker
First published in *Artemis Speaks*
by Nan Koehler

healing rituals
with children

Healing begins at the moment of birth—the unity of the mother and babe is maintained as she receives into her arms the fruit of her labor and loving. Usually in western culture, the tearing apart of this primary unit is the first step in a series of rituals which are, in fact, the opposite of healing.

Behind each and every ritual there is an important "frame of mind." Even if one is unaware of the symbolism of the ritual or its purpose, the enactment speaks to "pic-

tures" of the mind. We contain a whole gallery of these when it comes to our children, most of which hang unseen until their birth. As in any art show, if we know something about what we're viewing, our appreciation is deepened. And so the "framing" of these rituals, when done with care to harmonize with its essence, can be prepared beforehand and aesthetically enrich our experience of ritual. Birth is our first ex-

First published in "Special Delivery Newsletter," "Childbirth Alternatives Quarterly" and "Health and Happiness"; also excerpts from "Lotus Birth Fully Bloomed" originally published in THE WHOLE BIRTH CATALOG, edited by Janet Isaacs Ashford

perience in earthside ritual.

We prepare our consciousness for rituals with children by adopting this idea: Each and every baby is a very wise soul in a new body. All our babies are in a state of higher consciousness. Each one deserves great respect and is here to be honored, as we would honor a saint. Starting from this point of view, ritual becomes a holy experience.

My third pregnancy is begun, maintained and completed in ritual. Gannon, our first boy, is conceived during Anusthana, a ritual of yogis practiced five days preceding the full moon. Gannon was called by us, appropriately enough, on Earth Day of this ritual.

Let me share with you some of the healing rituals of this pregnancy, birth (in greater detail in "Emergence: First Son") and post-

partum. The delightful thing about being alive in the 20th century is that we are free to adapt, adopt and create from the world's treasury of rituals supportive for these feminine mysteries. To fully express who we are, as Americans in this example, draws upon our roots in the Judaeo-Christian, the AmerIndian and Yogic/Tantric cultures.

Other of our family rituals are pure inspiration (what we jokingly refer to as Mormon Tantra). Most conform to millenia-pure practice. Inspiration for two out of the three pregnancy rituals I will share here came from the MahaNirvana Tantras, how-to books which are thousands of years old. These rituals are to encourage growth and steward the sacred passage.

The first ritual is the conscious conception, where the divinities and holiness of creation itself is called forth. I will refer you to my title of that name for more information.

The second ritual is performed in the fifth month of gestation. This is from the MahaNirvana Tantra text refered to above. A supportive community of families is called to witness the asking of the divine architect to build a strong foundation.

A wise woman of the immediate community with living husband and children offers the pregnant mother sips of nectar (with a few grains in the bottom of the cup.) My cup-bearer was my friend Raven Lang. The nectar is somewhat likened to ''soma''—the divine food—and made of yogurt, milk, honey, ghee. To the carrier of the new babe she asks, ''And what do you want, oh gentle one, for this child?''

Classically in ancient India, the answer was for a son to help liberate his parents.

I answered with something to the effect for my child to realize who s/he really is.

A fire was built upon a yantra, or sacred geometric figure, and seeds were thrown into it (representing bad samskaras, or tendencies of negativity, past, present, future). The father of our baby recited seed sounds (bija) as he touched my heart and babe's heart and we all meditated together, chanted and generally had a lot of fun!

The next ceremony was done twice— Indian style both ways. Once in the Navajo way and the second time, as proscribed in the MahaNirvana Tantra, a ritual for house- holders before birth, East Indian style. The ceremony from the Navajo is called Blessing Way. This ritual was for my women

friends and children.

It took place in our mountain home, in our upstairs bedroom. My place of power— the bed Gannon was conceived in and would soon be birthed. My mother sat alongside as did the newest mother I had recently helped birth with her baby, my son's future friend. My dearest woman friend likewise sat close to me and I felt the power of the feminine with three generations of love surrounding me.

I was sung to, groomed, feet washed and rubbed with blue corn meal by my ''midwives''—my daughters and friend Nan Koehler. Then I was given gifts. This ritual is a welcoming one—it helps us know labor contractions as gifts and through the ritual we learn how to relax and receive all the at(tension). The ritual concluded with more songs sung by women birthing from all over the world. The AmerIndian version of a ''baby shower.''

The last ritual before Gannon's emergence was the tantric one for householders. Our spiritual community gathered to chant, give gifts and support our transition. This time the father of our coming baby, my lover, combed my hair traditionally with a golden comb and changed my hairstyle. In the Navajo cermony Blessing Way, a change in hairstyle, is also ritually practiced. My mother combed my hair in the Blessing Way. This prepared my head to change, from three to four children, a blended family. We realized that this baby was not just for our family, but our whole community. This is very healing—to make apparent the connections we share through having children.

The labor itself was ritual of a kind. Half of the time spent alone in meditation (two hours)—the other half on the bed Gannon was conceived in with papa helping support and sisters awaking at the very end to witness their brother's arrival. Healing of the tear began instantenously with our son's landing in mama and papa's arms together. I brought him to my heart immediately as his twin sisters reminded me to deliver the placenta.

Gannon's placenta was even named "Grandmother" by my girls. In HYGIEIA, my second book, I wrote about the Lotus Birth and our attempt at this new-age ritual with my twins' placenta.

With this birth, the lotus was fully bloomed. We saw the perfect balance of nature—as the new one, our son came into his body more fully, the old one, the placenta, left this world. When the third day postpartum arrived, the cord was quite crisp and the temptation to help its brittleness along was strong. However, we didn't cut the cord but allowed it to organically fall away. This waiting set the way for subsequent patience in letting old withered parts of the psyche drop off when their organic cycle was complete.

Lotus birth seemed to lay the template for a much more softer way than the heroic warrior with a sword (scissors) who cuts away, breaks through defenses and otherwise valiantly wounds the soul. We would allow our son's attachments to release when their own time was ripe, and the Lotus Birth was the initial testimony to that promise.

In the early afternoon of the third day, as the scent of placenta wafted richly around the redwood forest cabin, I noticed that the cord looked very different. It looked complete, full and ready to break forth. The old "Grandmother," Gannon's placenta rested in the Blessing Way bowl. This green ceramic bowl was given to me by my mother when I had my first kitchen away from her home. Now it lay on the bed with Gannon, our placenta and this bowl was connecting us three still. We honored Grandmother while she was with us but could see she wanted to rest in her mother, the earth, very soon. We burned cedar around our son's navel as incense. We watched, following closely.

Our son's cord came away from his navel with his family in attendance; the same loving mama, papa and sisters who were present at his birth. We all said it felt like his second birthing when the cord fell away.

Right then he seemed to purposefully grab
onto his dried cord. And as he grasped it,
slowly waving his arms, all the while holding
his newly released umbilical cord, we felt
honored to witness this rite of passage. A
few minutes later, seeming in very slow motion time, our newborn let go his cord and
each one of us experienced an incredible
energy rush. We felt his commitment to be
HERE at that moment, in his own time. Now
Gannon had given birth to himself.

   After the cord fell off three days
post-partum, we performed "Jata Karma"—
another ritual adopted form the MahaNirvana Tantra. His secret yogi name was
whispered into his ear and we gifted him

with a tiny piece of gold and silver. One each from the sun and the moon—his papa and mama, to wear around his neck in a "medicine bag." Also 12 flax seeds to help him grow beautiful were placed in the medicine bag. A crystal to soothe and some other little secrets and wishes for peace were made tangible and placed in his bag.

On the eighth day of Gannon's life earthside, the traditional time of circumcision (when the Vitamin K forms in newborn's bloodstreams—the clotting factor), we had another ritual. Needless to say we did not circumcise him. Instead we invited a pregnant couple to come sing welcoming songs and play music and annoint with bee pollen our son's third eye, soles, palms and belly. Visitors were few and invited to share with our babe what it is to be human in the most positive way.

Presentation to the Sun took place on the 22nd day. Up until this time, he was indoors—warm and snug with me. The ritual of mother-roasting was enacted (our room was kept very toasty with the help of papa's wood fires so that mother and baby could comfortably share their naked skin) and this along with plenty of special herbal teas precluded jaundice—which might be a problem when an infant is kept in diminishing semi-darkness for weeks. The Hopis as well as Hindus present the newborn to the Sun at the beginning of the third week with ceremony. At all times, the covering of the soft spot, or fontanelle, on top of the babe's head was observed when outdoors—another ritual honored in many parts of the world.

This was necessary until it closed several months later. Babies also lose heat from the top of the head, so this observance had another purpose—to keep the warmth of life in.

The first illness was accepted as a way to make the will-to-live stronger. As with death, sickness when not seen as the enemy, may actually serve higher consciousness. When the parents fear, they cannot see clearly what to do. Some tribes pulverize a piece of the dried umbilical cord and give the water to the sick baby. We smoked the room with cedar, prayed and affirmed our love for our baby. We also treated specifically the ailment with natural remedies. The healing ritual extended to uncovering the roots of the particular disease and making peace with the metaphor being expressed.

There are many more healing rituals we perform—some on a daily basis. Yet the common denominator of them all is TRUST. Trust that by our intention we are guiding our children ever more gently into the fullness of their being. And it is our children who teach us this trust and show us again and again that it is a basic human need to have someone to trust. What a blessing that we, as parents, are given this trust. It is by conscious rituals that we heal any doubt we might have to our worthiness as keepers of our children's health and happiness.

emergence: first son

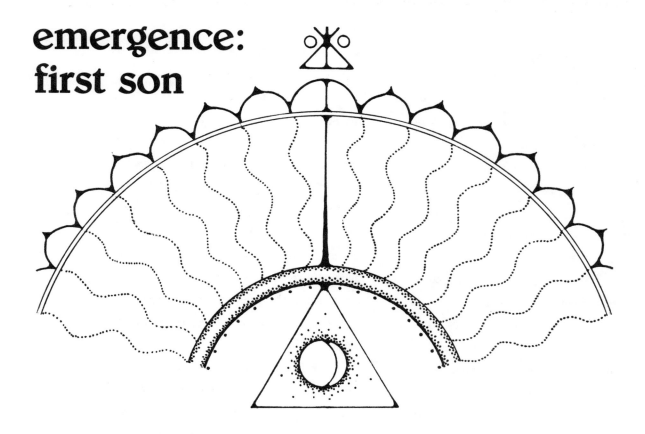

Birth Report of Gannon Hamilton
fourth-born, February 1, 1980
male, Aquarius ☉ Leo ☽

The birth stories of my first three children with other adults present, precedes the telling of our first born son; a do-it-yourself home-birth. I am struck with how much of my attention was focused on the doctor and hospital staff duing those births. I always thought that mothers tended to imprint on their helpers at births and, as midwife, I encouraged this bonding to take place within the family. Yet, in my own second and third deliveries, I did not focus on my husband— and this would later contribute to our divorce.

Five and one half years later I am re- married and pregnant with my fourth baby, and my present husband's first baby. The story of Gannon's birth begins in the Santa Cruz mountains of California.

I midwifed during my pregnancy and man- aged to include my husband in at a couple of births. One was a frank breech delivery. I felt he was prepared quite well. I trusted him more than any professional. I believe birth to be integral to the family's soul-making pro- cess, i.e., largely a psychological one. When

First published in *The New Nativity* Newsletter, edited by Marilyn Moran

the mother feels truly "safe" she delivers just fine. A doctor makes some women feel safe. Statistics lately don't bear this out as necessarily true but luckily for these mothers, doctors are plentiful and legal.

My last experience birthing twins at home had taught me that all the "safety" I needed was within. I didn't seek any medical or midwife care during this pregnancy and felt healthier for it.

Knowing the language of medical people and living in a medically oriented midwifery community, I was constantly challenged to explain my position of forsaking "experts" at my upcoming birth. My reply was that love got the baby going and love would help it come out. Besides, analyzing the word expert we discover that an "X" is a has-been, and a "spert" is a drip under pressure.

I imagined the birth, since it was my fourth baby and the previous twin birth had been painless, to be a love-making ritual between my husband and I. Privacy was needed for this. My daughters wanted to attend at the very end of the delivery. They had also been to a lot of births with me and had a reverent and natural attitude about it.

I never weighed myself, had my blood pressure taken, opened my legs to anyone but my lover, or had blood analyzed. I didn't pee into a jar and give away my waters to a laboratory. Instead, I looked within to find out what was happening. A regular meditation practice aided this. Each day I would sit still, quiet my mind, and commune with my baby as it grew. Breath was our primary "food."

I also ate impeccably, vegetarian and ayurvedic (literally meaning the science of life, health practices of yogis). No drinking, smoking and a lot of massage rounded out my prenatal yoga practice. A friend of my husband told him I looked like a shined apple. It was true—there was a glow! It was a special time in my life because my husband was so fresh to it all, and I was assured and peaceful. The combination proved to be delightful. He brought back all the wonder and I added the calming aura of experience, woman's wisdom: knowledge fallen into the heart.

The last week before delivery I went very "psychedelic." My perception altered and colors, sounds, textures and smells all seemed so vivid. Any little thing would send forth a gush of compassion. I felt so connected to this baby. When I would meditate with my baby my thoughts would almost stop completely as I imagined my baby's mind and mine being one; my baby didn't think at all—no chitt or thought waves yet in his mind. My baby was my guru or spiritual teacher. All the messages I received from this little one were positive. And, when two of my most trusted midwife friends said they thought my baby would just drop out of me, I felt blessed with ample support.

All of my babies had come just after the full moon. This baby followed in suit. Since I had bled so heavily on the last full moon birth, my husband was worried. I reminded him to tell me to "stop bleeding" if I were to hemorrhage and, just in case I should need them, I had all the herbal remedies

close by. He feared I might die. I told him that he couldn't get rid of me that easily and that it wasn't time for me to die.

I had many dreams about birth. I am Psyche's midwife, called by what I believe to be spirit to gently help babies into this world. So when I dreamed of birthing a baby with four arms, two of which became wings, I took it non-literally as a sign that psyche considered this baby an angel, amongst many possible meanings.

My little angel announced his forthcoming emergence during a full-moon meditation early in the evening. I had gone out to our meditation room and had an unusually visual focus throughout the hour I sat still. I kept seeing a tunnel with light at the end. Adding to the unoriginal tone, I kept hearing the song,

"I am a hollow bamboo, open up and let the light shine through" during my mindful time of silence.

As I returned to the bedroom, a beautiful scene met me. The girls were curled up in bed together listening to my husband read the Homeric Hymns. Just as I went into the bathroom I overheard the story of golden-hipped Aphrodite, the goddess of fertile sexuality, and Ganymedes, the cupbearer of the gods.

My cup is full, ready to be born; it spilleth over as I found the mucus plug has come out. I felt a rush of excitement and familiar downward "wind" or energy in my pelvis. I announced that our baby would be coming this night. The twins asked to be awakened at the very, very end. Being sea-

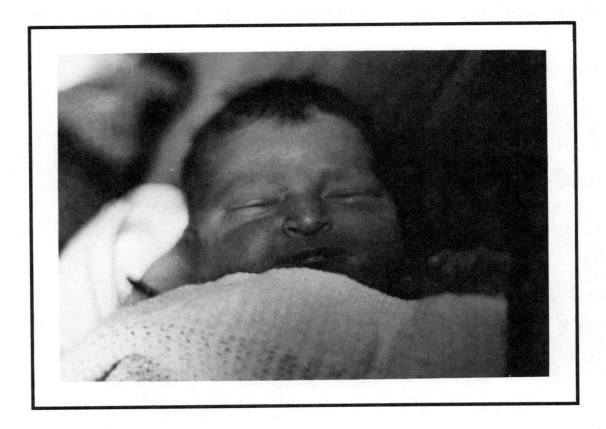

soned midwives, they didn't want to lose too much sleep waiting. They were so non-chalant about it that it made me laugh! I promised them and kissed the girls good-night.

A fantasy had claimed me about birthing—which was to do as much of labor and delivery alone as I could. After the twins' birth wherein I had many helping hands, I wanted to see what inner resources I had. I was quite romantic about it. I went to take a long bath by candlelight and very soon contractions began. I set up my birthing basket on the bed where our coming baby was conceived. And, being my own midwife, I journalled what was happening, pen in hand.

Within two hours my contractions

became quite heavy and fast. Through these two hours I meditated, moving about when my body needed to adjust a posture. I chose the poses which brought on the strongest contractions having long ago given up the notion that women have babies to get comfortable.

My ideal of delivering alone gave way to the need to have my husband, my lover hold me. The pressure became almost unbearable. I squatted over a bowl and found myself pushing. A big gush of water brought a sen-sation into my core which took my breath away. Then I knew what a BIG head feels like coming through the cervix. From that moment on I had one-pointed concentration, one mission: to get that baby out!

In less than four hours I had once again

gone from no contractions to full dilation. I felt my baby moving into my birth canal. I do not remember feeling very sexy at that time, and so another of my fantasies was left behind. I couldn't imagine making love with a big baby coming out of me (unless perhaps it would speed things along).

Everything seemed to move quickly from that first push. Each contraction (each gift) brought our baby down and with it more pain than I had prepared for. Isn't that the way with babies—we think we have prepared ourselves and then they come, turning us inside out and showing how little we indeed know ourselves after all.

My husband took his position bedside and soon our baby was crowning. I do remember him telling me to slow down. It seemed impossible and I forcefully pulled back my vulva with my own hands. Out popped the baby's head and I heard him sputtering his greeting as he slid into our waiting arms. I pulled him up to my breasts saying, "Oh my baby, my one." Roaring himself, he was in no need of clearing, massage or resuscitation. I think his quick deliverance got him going excellently. He had the roundest head!

Once again the placenta came right out and I began to hemorrhage. My husband said, "Ah, Jeannine, you're bleeding quite a lot. How about stopping?" I drank my herbal teas and stopped bleeding before any weakness or fainting took hold. Knowing of this tendency beforehand, I had concentrated my nutritive, herbal allies in pregnancy toward building an abundant and rich blood

supply. I have asked many people about my habit of hemorrhage at delivery. It remains a mystery. I think it has something to do with my need for attention and drama and leave it at that.

Looking back over my births, I see a progression which can best be summed up as becoming more conscious and more trusting to LET BE. The hospital drama during my twins' birth helped me to make peace with the medical perspective on birth and to know that I had nothing to fear there. Perhaps some "unfinished business" with hospitals led me there to discover how caring people are whether they dress in doctor's garb or not. The "do-it-yourself" homebirth was chosen not so much as a reaction AGAINST medicalized birthing, but for its own sake.

Actually I trust doctors more now for being so obvious about their beliefs. With midwives you never know if they will turn medical on you during a birthing. Unfortunately almost all midwives will rely on medical technique in an emergency. That is, midwives who have such training. And those midwives with state licenses are the most dangerous as they are bound legally to respond in crisis in a medical way. There are very few midwives I know, and I know A LOT of them having "un-trained" many through Hygieia College and touring the country speaking to birth audiences, whom I would trust to act harmlessly during a birth crisis.

I trusted my husband and bonded even deeper to him for having shared this birth so intimately and responsibly with me. I just knew in my heart of hearts that everything would be fine. I accepted that this baby was not coming FOR us, but THROUGH us. It was therefore a matter of getting out of his way. Whenever I remove selfish desires which limit my experience and accept what was meant to be, I always find the Truth.

If the twins' birth taught me to honor the primacy of my marriage bond during birth and allowed me to make peace with the medical belief system, then the birth of our first son carried me into a depth of compassion unknown before. I was turned inside out by the sensations of his birth. I have become a better midwife because of that pain with more understanding of how big babies can cause impatient behavior in the birthing mother. I used to be glib about the "pain" of delivery—to the point of calling any pain "optional" in birth. Gannon's emergence caused me to revision the value of pain in childbirth.

By pulling back my vulva at delivery, I created a midline perineal tear, a souvenir of my own impatience. Then I gained knowledge in how to naturally heal large tears. After four babies, this was my first big tear. I would still prefer my husband's hands to any others at my perineum, even if it meant more tearing at delivery. I also know now from the inside that tears do not need stitching if the tissue is healthy and helped along in its healing. A tear can actually improve one's sex life! Especially if painful stitching is refused and nature is trusted to heal. (More in PSYCHE'S MIDWIFE on this.)

After each birth I review my behavior in an attempt to learn from my experience and do better the next time. I have come to believe that childbirth is an art. Like other artistic expressions it becomes richer with more conscious practice and with discriminate incorporation of feed-back. I felt my twins' birth had been too big a community "happening" and my bonding got confused. After our son's birth I searched for things which were not ideal; for example my impatience and the resultant tearing. Although that did bring him to us at 4:00 A.M., "Brahma time," the best time for meditation when the mind is naturally calmest. I had hoped to feel more pleasure than pain at his birth. The ideal remains—a do-it-yourself homebirth that is spiritual, sexual and ecstatic. The mind is always finding ways to judge an experience as not perfect. It keeps the manifest world going in this way. However I am coming to accept this and know Gannon's birth has catalyzed great changes within and helped me to clarify my ideals in birth, and see them as that, IDEALS, and be content with what is. Each birth becomes "perfect" when seen this way.

As I grow older and attend with mature awareness more births, the number of beliefs I hold about childbirth decreases. There had been a seasoning of my attitude toward giving birth over the years. Birth has become synonymous with "mystery" or the "spirit." I know it is the greatest opportunity for women to know ourselves. The acceptance of birth as it naturally presents itself is a spir-

itual initiation. When shared in trust with our families, birth can bring an eternal bond between the mother and her loved ones. The more each mother reclaims her natural birthright the greater chance we will receive peace on our planet.

My story is shared with the hope that YOU will be inspired to trust the birthforce. your mate and your babies. By doing this, the gift we give our children is a balanced imprint of both sexes, mama and papa, as equal co-creators in life. Blessed be, gentle mothers and fathers everywhere.

the dolphin midwife

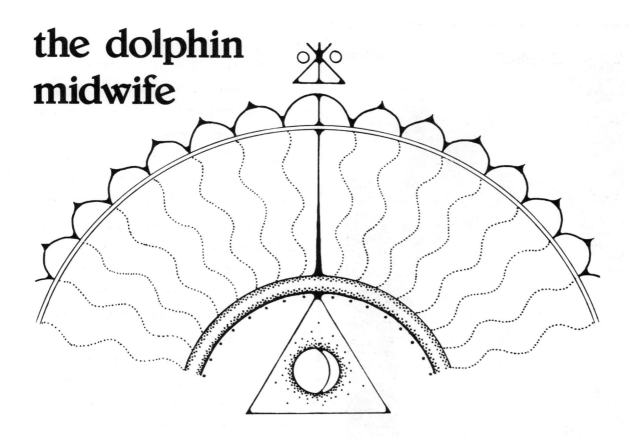

Birth Report of Quinn Ambriel
Fifth-born, June 11, 1984
male, Gemini ☉ Sagitarius ☽

Babies have never been a logical choice in my life. I hear the call of the child somewhere between estrogen and progesterone and begin the dialog.

"I need more time," my first opening. "There is no such thing as time here" the spirit voice, or pre-baby answers. From the soul's point of view there is no time. That is how hours can be spent in daydreaming, making love, meditating, etc., and it seems like an instant.

"We can't afford another baby," the rational, accountant mind responds. "I am coming to you not for what you will buy me" counters the pre-babe.

"I do really love you." My heart softens the edges of my mind. The argument is weakening. "My intention is not to make you poor, but to enrich your life beyond your hopes. I AM COMING TO SHOW YOU WHAT YOUR LOVE LOOKS LIKE."

Tracking our baby Quinn's first signal to us that he was ready to be conceived

First published in *Children of the Dawn* by Joshua Halpern; also printed in *Conscious Conception: Elemental Journey through the Labyrinth of Sexuality* by Jeannine Parvati Baker, Frederick Baker and Tamara Slayton

would have been difficult were it not for an unforgettable experience. This memory is somatically burned into me on the deepest level.

Just previous, I had been aware of our next baby around the skirts of imagination, waiting patiently for his parents to begin the creation dance.

However, we were struggling financially with our book *Conscious Conception,* tending our growing family with little support for another baby. Even my own mother, already a grandmother four times over, resisted another grandchild. "Why you could be famous, Jeannine, if you'd stop having babies already!"

"But Mom, I'm already famous with God."

Around the time of this dialog, I suffered a serious burn accident in a sauna. I sustained third, second and first degree burns and convalesced for many weeks doing meditation.

I understood that knowing pain was integral to developing my healing powers for others. But the usual way "medicine women" acquire this knowledge through giving unmedicated birth was not my experience. Giving birth has never been excruciating for me. I wouldn't voluntarily inflict suffering upon myself either by joining a heroic medicine society and being initiated into the mysteries of healing through pain. And so I have skimmed through life without any direct knowledge of outrageous pain. (As reflected by my own drugged delivery, I was birthed through an anesthesized woman and subsequently skillfully avoided excruciation the rest of my life.) These thoughts helped somewhat to cope with the searing pain which lasted weeks. But it was my relationship with Quinn as our pre-baby which was my greatest ally in forgoing pharmaceutical drugs or being admitted into a burn center/hospital for escape from pain.

During the height of my agony I heard Quinn's strong voice. "Stay alive Mom! Don't give up! You can pull through the pain. I love you." When the burning hurt the most I could sometimes go out of my body (that is, disengage from feeling attached to the body) and it was in those altered states

lovers do so well. It had been a long separation for us—almost three weeks apart. There was change afoot in several ways, not the least being the offer to caretake a secluded Hawaiian home/pyramid for the winter. My preference was to go home to Utah and conceive our baby. Yet we chose to begin our next pregnancy "in transit"—the favored way of Geminis.

The night of Quinn's conception was a soothing one. All seemed in order, which is

that Quinn came through loud and clear.

The thought of conceiving another baby with my husband was the most inspiring idea "to hang in there" as I lay in tremendous agony. I credit my quick recovery to the high spirits maintained behind this fantasy of becoming pregnant once more.

After recovery was complete and I could walk again, Quinn became a constant companion. He told me many things through the feminine spirit voice. Preparations for birth as vision quest came through this voice that we had named "Hermione", messenger-goddess to the Greeks. Perhaps Quinn chose a male form in part to escape this naming! In any case, when Rico and I began our preparations to conceive Quinn, it was under the guidance of Hermione, and with no preference for either male or female baby.

With the romance of the universe in effect, we had a rendezvous during a teaching tour I was making along the coast of California. Rico met me, fittingly enough, in a private sauna at a midwife-friend's home in Santa Cruz. We sparked in the way old

the original meaning of the word "cosmic". Excitement generated by our decision to move to Hawaii (and miss one of the coldest winters on record in Utah) added to the anticipation of the unknown. Our ordinary miracle was about to begin.

WE OPENED UP BODY-PRAYER TOGETHER.

The mouths unfurl. All eyes turn together. Legs entwine the private parts. Skin

grows slippery. Fingers in love mudras. Our breath slows, then rapids. River of ecstasy. Hopes spilling over. Filling and emptying again and again. Swirlingly still. We're riding

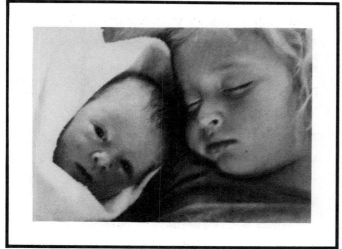

the standing wave. And he is praying aloud with me.

"Dear Divine Parents, we are so grateful for Thy presence and infinite love. We thank Thee for this blessing of sexuality and the forms through which we worship Thee. Most kind Heavenly Father and Mother, we are humbled by Thy creation and are filled with awe at Thy power. We thank Thee for all our children, those here with us now, those who have already left the nest, and those yet to fly home to us. We thank Thee for our precious parents and all our ancestors who have given us this gift of life. And most happily we thank Thee for this lover, here, our mate. The One through whom we can touch Thee.

We ask Thee to guide and bless this conception so that it may be pleasing unto Thee. LET THY WILL BE DONE EMBODIED AS IT IS IN SPIRIT. We ask Thee to bring great health, intelligence, strength, and wisdom to us so that this child can always be close to Thee and live Thy ways with fullness of joy. Please grant this being the knowledge of its source. LET THIS BABY SERVE THEE IN ALL WAYS.

We say these things in the names of all Thy great teachers and Thy beloved son Jesus Christ, our ultimate healer, who have come to earth to show us who we really are.

Amen, Blessed Be, and HO!''

WE PRAY QUINN INTO EXISTENCE. MY SECRET HOPE OUR BABY WILL ALWAYS KNOW THIS LOVE, FEEL THIS LOVE THAT BROUGHT HIM HERE IN THE FIRST PLACE.

A few days later our passion is heightened and the heat is on! The inner nest is building and fresh hope dwells in the soul. Along with teaching we also play—a night at the dance hall is up for us. Children settled in with friends we fly off to the civic auditorium for reggae dancing. A night at the concert opening our bodies up for sublime surrender. Let the music carry us blissward! During the ecstatic opening of the headliners, I HAVE A VISION AS I FEEL MY WOMB SURFACE THE SKIN OF MY SEX.

The space shuttle arrives on the moon. The earth receives the watered seed. The cell inlets another protein. A new idea is accepted. The sister joins the sorority, hazing complete. The mother opens her arms up to her child, hugging closest. The jellyfish eats. The net catches the flying artist. The orchestra finishes tuning up. The lovers reach second base. The ball makes it through the basket. The yeast falls into the bread. I AM

BAKERWOMAN GOD. The zygote implants in the uterus.

That night I dream of burying myself into warm sand. There is a cluster of sisters about me. They are chanting "into the ring of mugwort". Mugwort, the sacred totem plant of Artemis, goddess of the wilderness in birth. Mugwort, the herb we burn as incense to see into the FUTURE—another metaphor of the new one, our baby to be. Sisters clustered, like so many eggs ripening in various degrees of maturation. Eggs who might become sisters, sisters who came from eggs.

I am participating in some ritual, some woman mystery and these sisters are helping me matriculate. The feeling is a sacred one and I personally am very honored to be accepted into the fold.

THE PELVIS KNOWS. THESE HIPS HOLD MAGIC. THE DREAM CONFIRMS WHAT IS ALREADY FELT. I AM PREGNANT, IMPLANTED AND WILL WALK THE MOTHER'S PATH AGAIN.

Change still afoot, we move our entire home business from Utah to Hawaii for the pregnancy. Gestating in the tropical rain forest without the creature comforts of civilization, but with lots of jungle creatures. Since we had no electricity, it was to bed when the sun goes down and up before dawn. We breathe clean Pacific Ocean air. We swim in crystal blue ocean and drink pure rainwater. In Hawaii I grow to love water even more as a powerful purification. I often imagine when floating in the ocean and riding waves that I am like my baby now,

surrounded and sustained by salty water. Along the way we discover that paradise is a state of mind.

While in Hawaii, I attend midwife meetings and learn about underwater birth. The closest I had come to witnessing an underwater birth before was during a precipitous birth I attended as midwife. When I arrived in the birthing home, the mother in labor was grunting HARD as she sat on the toilet.

This was NOT the kind of underwater birth I supported.

There is a rich heritage of birthing tidepools for the islanders. I hear about Australian, French and Russian women who birth their babies underwater. Sometimes dolphins swim close by and act as midwives. I am more than intriqued—I AM ATTRACTED TO THIS CONCEPT BEYOND LOGIC, JUST AS I WAS OPEN TO THIS FIFTH BABY FOR REASONS BEYOND "COMMON SENSE".

I have no fear of birth. That's a gift as well as an earned trust. From the moment the bloody show comes, I know my babies will arrive within several hours. All my other babies have been born on the full moon (or within hours). How did I know the deliveries would be graced? The same way that I knew I was pregnant so early on. The brain-heart knows. And once the monkey-mind quiets down enough, all the information we need is right here, within.

Now to practice the inward skills once again. We are back home in Utah, just

finishing un-packing. It is a sunny and clear day. Rico is working in our basement, our home office of Freestone Innerprizes. I have just written a letter to Marilyn Moran, author of BIRTH AND THE DIALOG OF LOVE, my favorite birth book this pregnancy. I feel the bloody show slip through.

This is my first labor in the daytime. All four babies previously had initiated their labors at midnight and come before or just at dawn. IT SEEMED SO NAKED, SO OBVIOUS TO GIVE BIRTH IN THE DAYTIME. I SUBMERGE ALL MODESTY AND GIVE MYSELF TO BIRTH.

Being the empiricist that I am, I must try the various stages of labor in and out of the water bath. Does the water really help? In earlier labor there seemed to be little dif-

ference. Except that I can more easily kiss and hug my family on dry land than in our tiny bathtub. But once we move towards transition, I note a marked change out of the water. The gifts become LABOR PAINS, out of the bath, while in the warm water the birthforce JUST FEELS STRONG. Even up to the second stage I am getting in and out of the tub to feel the difference. Each time I carefully wash my feet to keep the water clean. Oh yes, THE WATER DEFINITELY HELPS TRANSFORM PAIN INTO URGENT PRESSURE.

Gannon, now four years old, comes into the tub at transition. He squirts a rubber dolphin bathtub toy at me. We giggle together. I have my dolphin midwife after all!

I feel the baby come down. The sensation is ecstatic. I had prepared somewhat for this being painful as my last delivery had been. Yet this time the pulse of birth feels wonderful! I am building up to the birth climax after nine months of pleasureable foreplay. With one push the babe is in the canal. THE NEXT PUSH BRINGS HIM DOWN, DOWN INTO THAT SPACE JUST BEFORE ORGASM WHEN WE WOMEN KNOW HOW GOD MUST HAVE FELT CREATING THIS PLANET.

The water supports my birth outlet. I AM NO LONGER ALONE IN THIS WORK. I FEEL CONNECTED TO THE MAINLAND, TO MY SOURCE. THESE MIDWIFE HANDS KNOW JUST WHAT TO DO TO SUPPORT THE NOW CROWNING HEAD, coming so fast. How glad I am for all those years of orgasms! Slow orgasms, fast ones, those which build and subside and peak again and again. That practice aids my baby's gentle emergence so that he doesn't spurt out too quickly. HE COMES, AS DO I.

I slip my fingers around his neck, and what's this? Ah, a little hand. I hold back this hand as he rotates and delivers first one shoulder, then the other. OUT SLIPS OUR BABY INTO HIS PARENTS HANDS. HE SWIMS RIGHT INTO OUR HEARTS.

Some water babies stay submerged after delivery for minutes but mine wanted to come to the surface immediately. He turns and faces me, eyes shut, and says, "Lift me up!"

I pull my baby up to the surface and drape a towel over his head. Gradually he opens one eye, then the other to gaze in

wonder. He isn't breathing perceptibly so I hug him all the closer and sing the welcoming song. He is warm and his color is coming on so I do not worry as we await his first perceptible breath. I kiss his face, gently sucking out the mucus in his airways through his nose and mouth. We ADORE him.

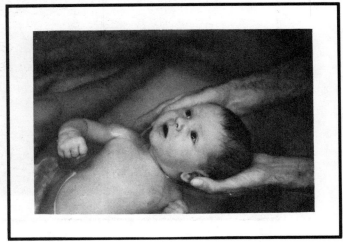

The placenta, or the "Grandmother" as we like to call our babies' first mother, delivers itself minutes later. How easy clean-up is when birthing in the bathtub! Most all the blood clots fall to the bottom of the tub, whose water is bright red now. I RECALL THE STORY OF MOSES AND THE PARTING OF THE RED SEA. MY POST-PARTUM BODY FEELS AS IF MOSES HAD JUST BEEN THROUGH ME WITH THE CHOSEN ONES.

Was it the water which made this birth so ecstatic and sexually fulfilling? I would like to shout, "IT'S THE WATER!" but must admit, only possibly so. It is a lot easier for me to interpret the birthforce as blissful gifts when contractions don't hurt. Yet in all

honesty, I don't really know for sure. This is the way it is with birth—it doesn't lend itself to repeatable experiment well. Each birth is totally unique. I just remember that when Quinn came into my birth canal there was no way I would forsake the comfort of the bath.

In closing, let me say that it is a pity that we women quit having babies just when we are getting good at giving birth. This last childbirth I did have my vision quest fulfilled. At Quinn's emergence I SAW every woman on this earth giving birth like I was doing—in ecstasy, with her lover and in the sanctity of home. To this vision, I pledge my total committment.

Wishing YOU a blissful birthing in all ways.

beginnings, again

Blessed afterword! As this new edition goes to press we are pregnant with baby number six. This was a truly cosmic conception as our new one rode in on the tail of Halley's comet.

With deepest gratitude and humility ensouling our family, we ponder our abundance. God must love me very much, especially knowing so well all my faults, to trust me again with another precious spirit.

When I wrote my yoga teacher Baba Hari Dass about this new one in the oven at the Alchemical Bakery, he replied, "You're Tantric Sadhana is working. The union of Shiva and Shakti is creation."

I also thanked him for the previous advice to concentrate on my navel chakra during labor as this transformed labor pains into the gifts they really are. Absolutely no pain birthing Quinn! Now that birth was less of a personal vision quest for me, and more for the spirituality of the new one, I asked him how and where I might concentrate to help this coming baby retain higher consciousness as she arrives planetside. He answered with words to the effect of all the preceding ones in this book. Each moment, especially in pregnancy, think of spiritual things and BE that higher consciousness myself—that will imprint the baby with spirituality as she comes through birth's door.

And so gentle ones, like you I am vulnerable to the unknown once more. God-Us only knows how this birth will come out "in the end." My faith is strong and as you read know I am saying a prayer for your blissful birthing—now please say a prayer for mine. It is the beginning, again.

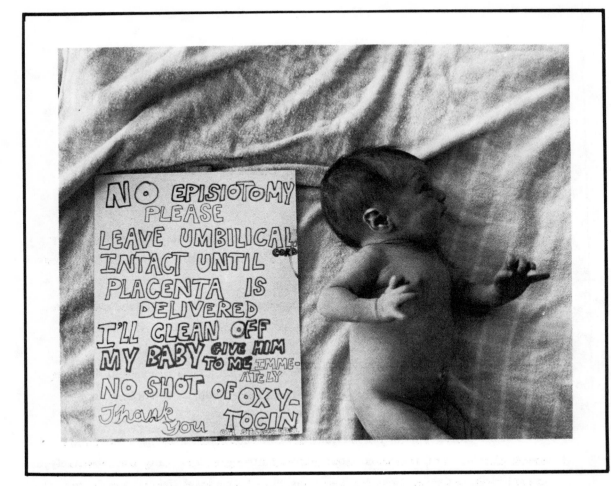

Preferred Books to Read

Nature's Children by Julliette De Bairacli Levy. Schocken Books, New York. Published in Great Britain, 1970. LCC no. 78–163326.

Two Births by Brown, Lesser, Mines and Buryn. Random House and Bookworks, New York and Berkeley, 1972.

Childbirth Is Ecstasy by Allen Cohen and Stephen Walzer. Aquarius Publishing Co., San Francisco, 1971.

Birth Book by Raven Lang. Big Trees Press, Felton, California, 1972.

Touching: The Significance of Human Skin by Ashley Montagu. Columbia University Press, 1971.

The Growth and Development of Mothers by Angela Barron McBride. Harper and Row, 1973.

The Feeling Child by Arthur Janov. Simon and Schuster, 1973.